Precious Children of
MYANMAR

Register This New Book

Benefits of Registering*

- ✓ FREE **replacements** of lost or damaged books
- ✓ FREE **audiobook** – *Pilgrim's Progress*, audiobook edition
- ✓ FREE information about new titles and other **freebies**

www.anekopress.com/new-book-registration

*See our website for requirements and limitations.

Precious Children of
MYANMAR

Giving Voice to Destitute Children of the World

ELIZABETH A. CARPENTER
PHOTOGRAPHY BY BRUCE M. CARPENTER

We love hearing from our readers. Please contact us at www.anekopress.com/questions-comments with any questions, comments, or suggestions.

Precious Children of Myanmar
© 2020 by Elizabeth A. Carpenter
All rights reserved. Published 2020.

No part of this book may be reproduced, stored in a retrieval system, or transmitted in any form or by any means – electronic, mechanical, photocopying, recording, or otherwise, without written permission from the publisher.

Scripture quotations marked (NIV) are taken from the Holy Bible, New International Version®, NIV®. Copyright © 1973, 1978, 1984, 2011 by Biblica, Inc.® Used by permission of Zondervan. All rights reserved worldwide. www.zondervan.com The "NIV" and "New International Version" are trademarks registered in the United States Patent and Trademark Office by Biblica, Inc.®

Scripture quotations also from The Authorized (King James) Version. Rights in the Authorized Version in the United Kingdom are vested in the Crown. Reproduced by permission of the Crown's patentee, Cambridge University Press.

Cover Design: Jonathan Lewis
Cover Image: Myanmar street boys photographed by Bruce Carpenter
Editors: Sheila Wilkinson and Ruth Clark

Printed in the United States of America
Aneko Press
www.anekopress.com
Aneko Press, Life Sentence Publishing, and our logos are trademarks of
Life Sentence Publishing, Inc.
203 E. Birch Street
P.O. Box 652
Abbotsford, WI 54405

RELIGION / Christian Ministry / Children
Paperback ISBN: 978-1-62245-684-0
eBook ISBN: 978-1-62245-685-7

10 9 8 7 6 5 4 3 2 1

Available where books are sold

Contents

Acknowledgments vii

Introduction ix

Ch. 1: Mang Lian Hup 1

Ch. 2: Mai Jar 23

Ch. 3: Mala 35

Ch. 4: Khuang Ja 49

Ch. 5: Lang Meng and Cin Vang 61

Ch. 6: Dua Lian Hmung 69

Ch. 7: Seng Nu 77

Ch. 8: Sung Tha Chin 89

Ch. 9: Thang Duh Lian 101

Ch. 10: Mang Lian Hup's A Phua 109

Child Help International 119

About the Author 121

This book is dedicated to our Savior and Deliverer, Jesus, and to the precious children of Myanmar.

For he will deliver the needy who cry out, the afflicted who have no one to help. He will take pity on the weak and the needy and save the needy from death. He will rescue them from oppression and violence, for precious is their blood in his sight. (Psalm 72:12-14 NIV)

Acknowledgments

First, we thank God for the privilege of going to Myanmar to work with His children. These precious children are the future of this country that has a history of unrest and hostility. Working with these children who have faced tremendous challenges in their short lives has inspired us.

We want to thank our family, friends, and church family for giving us so much love and support as we prepared and traveled on this story-gathering mission trip.

Also, we want to thank the missionaries whom we are honored to work with again at Child Help International – Nate, Stacy, and the Myanmar teams.

We could not have done this project without the prayers and support of our board members – Dave, Theresa, Naomi, Kathy, and Bonnie, and of course, our supporters who gave generously to send us on this mission.

We thank all the precious children of Myanmar who were brave enough to share the good and the bad of your lives. Your strength, courage, dreams, and faith during difficult situations humbled and inspired us. Our love and prayers will be with you always.

Finally, we thank you for reading about the experiences of these precious children and listening to their voices.

In His Service,
Elizabeth & Bruce

Introduction

This book is a different format from past *Precious Children* books because we must protect the location and identities of the children, staff, and missionaries that we worked with in Myanmar. After prayerful consideration, we chose to share their stories through the brave women who rescued them and took them to the Christian children's homes in Myanmar. These stories are depicted as they were told to us by the children we interviewed. This book is based on a compilation of firsthand interviews, file documentation, and cultural research. By telling the story through the eyes of a fictional woman who represents several real Christian women who work to rescue the children, we will introduce you to the lives of these precious children. Because Myanmar is still under military rule, and protection of these homes is a sensitive issue, we have done everything we can to share their stories while concealing everyone involved who supports them in Myanmar. All names and locations have been changed to achieve this security.

The hardest part of this mission field is the delicate balance between following the military government rules and protecting/providing for these rescued Christian children. These Christian children's homes are closely monitored by the government. The pastors and staff at the homes walk a fine line to make sure they are not breaking the law while raising Christian children. Our readers will notice these stories are shorter than the ones we have shared in previous books. Due to the military watching our activity, we had limited time with the children. The children were afraid to talk with us because they were interrogated by military officials when they came to the home. They are photographed and monitored while they live in the children's home. We interviewed them in a room where we were not noticed, so we only had a couple hours with each child. We were blessed to have enough time to talk with each child twice.

The pastors told us that as a whole, many people in Myanmar are very private. The children did not open up easily, and we learned much of each child's story from the notes in their files and from the staff who cared for the children. Something that each child talked about was about being rescued and brought to the children's homes. They talked about the women who traveled with them and how they journeyed across the country. For many of them this was the first time they were out of their villages, and it was scary and exciting. That led us to feature these courageous women through the character "Sui Zi" in our book. She is a representation of what each child shared with us.

In order to protect the children, we made the tough decision to eliminate any photographs of the children or the areas in which we traveled. The missions we worked with gave us permission to show the children if we did it in black and white and masked their faces. The government in Myanmar takes pictures of all the children in the homes, and facial recognition software could be used to identify the children and the homes with which we worked. The Myanmar government does not want uncontrolled news leaving their country. For these reasons we decided to show no photographs of these precious children. We will be glad to share pictures in our speaking engagements and with our partner churches upon request. Our contact information is at the end of this book if you are

INTRODUCTION

interested in hearing directly from us and seeing the pictures that go with these stories.

There are many cultural terms used in this book which are defined below for quick reference.

Mih Khin – Mother

Phan Khin – Father

A Phua – Grandmother

A Bo – Grandfather

Standard – Grade in school

Tuition Class – Tutoring

Kyauk Pyin – A stone that is used to grind thanaka paste

Thanaka – A type of wood that is ground to make thanaka paste

Thanaka Paste – A dough-like mixture that is used in Myanmar to apply to faces, believed to help cool them in the hot climate. Women apply it in decorative designs while men apply it in lines or circles.

Longyi – A sheet of cloth widely worn in Myanmar (formerly Burma), approximately 6.6 feet long and 2.6 feet wide and often sewn into a cylindrical shape. It is worn around the waist, running to the feet, and held in place by folding the fabric over without a knot. It is sometimes folded up to the knee for comfort.[1]

KIA – The Kachin Independence Army is a non-state group and the military wing of the Kachin Independence Organization (KIO), a political group of ethnic Kachins in northern Myanmar. The Kachins are a coalition of six tribes whose homeland encompasses territory in Yunnan, China, northeast India, and

---

[1] www.en.wikipedia.org/wiki/Longyi, accessed December 16, 2019.

Kachin State in Myanmar. The Kachin Independence Army is funded by the KIO, which raises money through regional taxes and trade in jade, timber, and gold. Its rifles are a combination of AK-47s, homemade rifles (such as KA-07s), and some artillery. Kachin Independence Army headquarters are in Laiza, in southern Kachin State near the Chinese border. In October 2010, KIA commanders said that they had ten thousand regular troops and ten thousand reservists. In May 2012, the group had about eight thousand troops. The Kachin Independence Army members are mostly militants. The KIA is designated as a terrorist group by the Myanmar government. The Kachin people are known for their disciplined fighting skills, complex clan interrelations, craftsmanship, herbal healing, and jungle survival skills. The greatest number of Kachin people live in Myanmar (roughly one million).[2]

Tatmadaw – The official name of the armed forces of Myanmar. It is administered by the Ministry of Defense and composed of the army, the navy, and the air force. Auxiliary services include the Myanmar Police Force and the People's Militia Units. According to the Constitution of Myanmar, the Tatmadaw directly reports to the National Defense and Security Council (NDSC). The NDSC is an eleven-member National Security Council responsible for security and defense affairs in Myanmar. The NDSC serves as the highest authority in the government of Myanmar.[3]

---

[2] www.en.wikipedia.org/wiki/Kachin_Independence_Army, accessed December 16, 2019.
[3] www.en.wikipedia.org/wiki/Tatmadaw, accessed December 16, 2019.

Mang Lian Hup

After the five-hour train ride, Sui Zi left the station, thankful to stretch her legs. The local pastor welcomed her and her husband, inquired about their well-being, and proceeded to tell her about the family they would meet. As they drove to the village, he said, "The *a phua* (grandmother) you will meet loves her grandson very much, but she is not able to adequately care for him."

The *mih khin* (mother) had abandoned both of her sons, seven-year-old Mang Lian Hup and his eleven-year-old brother, Cung Nawl Sung, to be cared for by their aging *a phua*. "About a year ago, the *a phua* sent the older boy to live with her sister on a larger farm where he could work and attend school," the pastor continued. "I believe the *a phua* is a widow in her late sixties, so she is unable to provide for food, clothing, and school for Mang Lian Hup as she had hoped."

The Kachin Christian churches had notified the pastor and asked for help for the *a phua* and Mang Lian Hup. As they drove the dusty, sixty-minute trip to the *a phua*'s village, Sui Zi prayed for God's guidance on how to best help Mang Lian Hup. She knew there was an opening at one of the Christian children's homes that she worked with in Mandalay – Hope Christian Children's Home. Her purpose in this trip was to see if Mang Lian Hup would be a good fit for the home and if the *a phua* wanted him to go. Sui Zi asked God to make His will clear to them and guide their discussion that day.

As the dust settled, they exited the car and walked toward the *a phua*'s hut. The pastor pointed out the strawberry farm next to the village where the *a phua* and Mang Lian Hup worked. As they approached the hut, he waved to Mang Lian Hup, a little boy running and playing with other boys. Sui Zi noticed how small Mang Lian Hup was, but he had a smile that lit up his entire face. His eyes sparkled, and he looked happy. They called out a greeting and entered the *a phua*'s hut where she sat on a mat.

Strips of bamboo that the *a phua* had cut for weaving surrounded her. Her bamboo baskets would be used to carry the strawberries to market during the harvest. As they entered the hut, Mang Lian Hup's *a phua* stopped her work and carefully got up to receive them. She appeared tired but welcomed them with a smile.

Sui Zi took both of her hands in her own and greeted her in the name of Jesus. "Please sit and join me for tea while the pastor attends to other needs in the village," the *a phua* responded.

They sat together and the *a phua* poured each of them a cup. "Do you mind if I continue to weave baskets as we talk? These baskets provide our money for food." The two women talked about life in the village and their faith in God.

"How are you and Mang Lian Hup getting along?" Sui Zi asked.

"By the grace of God, we have just enough food from our work in the fields and a bit more from weaving baskets. I am so sad that I cannot afford to send him to school. I can only work enough to care for one of the boys. I am not able to provide enough to care for both of them. I am too old to work all day in the fields, so I weave baskets for the strawberry harvest," the *a phua* shared with Sui Zi. She only earned enough for tea, rice, and some vegetables to feed them.

"I understand farm life," Sui Zi told the older woman, "and it is difficult to work in the fields as we age. Tell me about Mang Lian Hup."

The *a phua* paused in her work, blew into her tea, and watched the steam, as if she saw the memories in the steam. "It is a sad story that breaks my heart to share. I love Mang Lian Hup and he is my joy and the spark that keeps me going every day. Mang Lian Hup was born seven years ago to my youngest daughter and son-in-law. They lived here on the farm and worked the strawberry fields. Mang Lian Hup is their second son; his older brother was four years old when Mang Lian Hup was born. I spent my days watching the boys, cooking, and making the bamboo strawberry baskets while my daughter and her husband worked the fields.

"We were very blessed that the land owner paid a fair wage and treated his workers well. Once a month he shared meat with the families who worked his farm, and he planned the workweek to allow the families to attend the village church every Sunday.

"I wish I could say it was a happy time, but my son-in-law became addicted to alcohol. He drank more and more and was not satisfied with the life of a sharecropper. By the time Mang Lian Hup was four, his father worked much less in the fields and spent the family's money on alcohol. One day he did not come home. We learned that he was killed for the debt he owed to the bootleggers.

"All Mang Lian Hup remembers of his father is that he was a drunkard and did not work as hard as the rest of the family. My daughter was devastated at the loss of her husband and remarried quickly, as is common for most widows in the village. Mang Lian Hup was five at that time."

The *a phua* sighed and told Sui Zi that her daughter is unlucky in her choice of husbands. "The new husband worked hard in the fields but was quick to discipline them very harshly with severe beatings, especially the two boys. He forced me to move into my own hut, away from my daughter and grandchildren, because he did not like me around. He forced me to live on my own, so I had to work full-time in the fields to care for myself. My grandsons would visit my hut to escape the harshness of their stepfather. Sometimes he would come and yell at them to get back to their home. All happiness left my daughter's eyes with this new husband. When she found herself with child, the stepfather became even more harsh with Mang Lian Hup and his brother.

"One day he beat Mang Lian Hup so severely that my daughter took both boys and brought them to me. She begged me to take her sons and protect them. She told me that she and her husband were leaving the village because he wanted a new start in another part of Kachin State where he had heard there was good work. I begged my daughter to leave this husband and stay with me and the boys, but she said she could not leave her husband because she was carrying his child and she had to leave her sons to make him happy. My daughter believed she had to honor her husband and stay with him to protect the boys."

Sui Zi watched the sadness on the *a phua*'s face as she talked of her daughter abandoning her children for the honor of this husband and his new life. She was hurt at the loss of her daughter and even more hurt about the children being left behind. She took a long breath, collected herself, and continued.

"I thought my daughter truly believed she was protecting the boys from this harsh man who beat them. Both boys were glad to be away from him and adjusted to their mother leaving. Mang Lian Hup was six and his brother was ten. I praise God for the boys not being upset; I worried that they would be scarred by their mother leaving them.

"For three months all three of us worked as hard as we could around the strawberry farm. Mang Lian Hup and his brother weeded the rows of strawberries and cut the grass. The boys gathered bamboo for me to cut into strips and weave into baskets. I helped in the fields and wove baskets as much as my hands could handle. Even with all three of us working, we barely had enough money for tea, rice, and vegetables. Mang Lian Hup and his brother sometimes caught fish for us to eat. The landowner's monthly gift was usually the only other meat we had."

The *a phua* felt bad that she could not afford to send the boys to school. "I do not have funds to provide them with the uniforms, books, or supplies that they need for school. When my youngest sister, who lives in another part of Kachin State, was visiting, I told her she could take one of the boys. Her family could send him to school, and he could help them by working on their farm. I decided to send Cung Nawl Sung, the older boy, because I could not bear to lose Mang Lian Hup.

"Mang Lian Hup was very sad to see his brother and best friend leave. Cung Nawl Sung had taught him many things, like how to play futbal (football), fish for food, and catch the small fish in the creek to keep in plastic bottles as pets. Mang Lian Hup was so happy when I took him on the three-hour trip to see his brother."

Filled with compassion and empathy, Sui Zi listened and realized that the *a phua* deeply loved Mang Lian Hup and would have a difficult time parting with him. He was her joy and gave her purpose in life.

With a heavy heart she explained how hard she worked to support him; it was very difficult. When the pastor suggested she meet with Sui Zi, her first thought was that she could not possibly go on without her little Mang Lian Hup. Then she considered how much a growing boy eats and needs, and that he would continue to grow taller and need new clothes. She couldn't even afford to send him to school. If he could go to school, maybe he'd get a better job and be able to care for himself and someday her. The thought of these things made her agree to see Sui Zi. As they discussed the current hardships, Sui Zi listened to the *a phua*'s deep desire for Mang Lian Hup to obtain an education and get a good job.

Sui Zi then told the *a phua* about Hope Christian Children's Home in Mandalay. She assured her that she had helped several children from Kachin State relocate to the home and knew firsthand of the care they were given. She said, "The pastor who runs the home makes sure the children have food, clothing, medical care, and an education. They go to church and study the Bible. Other boys and girls in the home are the same age as Mang Lian Hup; they could be playmates and friends."

Still hoping to stay with Mang Lian Hup, the *a phua* asked, "Is there any way I can go with Mang Lian Hup and work in the home?"

"I'm afraid the house staff is all in place with no opportunities to work at the home," Sui Zi responded. "Even I live in Kachin State and only travel with children to Mandalay to place them in the home. I stay for two to three days with the children when I place them so they have a familiar face for a few days. When I take new children to the home, I always look forward to visiting the ones I've already placed there. I would be glad to bring you news of Mang Lian Hup from those trips." Sui Zi knew this would be a tough decision for the *a phua* but asked if she could meet Mang Lian Hup. The *a phua* slowly rose, whether from hesitation or stiff joints from sitting for hours making strawberry baskets, it was not clear.

A Phua called Mang Lian Hup in to meet Sui Zi and have lunch. She introduced Sui Zi as a lady who helps young children like him. He looked confused but was glad to get something to eat. Sui Zi saw how much he loved his *a phua* and how she loved caring for him. *A Phua* gave him a large serving of rice and vegetables and then offered Sui Zi some lunch, which she declined. She had brought her lunch bucket, so she would not stress the limited food supply of the *a phua*. She had packed only rice and vegetables because that would be the food they ate in the village. Sui Zi noticed that the *a phua* served herself a meager serving to save more food for her grandson.

During lunch Sui Zi asked Mang Lian Hup, "What do you like to play? Do you have some favorite things?"

He said, "I want to be a famous futball player when I grow up."

Sui Zi smiled and asked him, "What would you do as a famous futball player?"

He answered, "I will make a lot of money and take care of *A Phua*. And red is my favorite color because that is the color of the uniform of my favorite futball team. I like to eat boiled chicken because the landowner gives us chicken every month, and I like how *A Phua* boils it for me."

As they talked, Sui Zi noticed that Mang Lian Hup did not speak Burmese but rather Jingpho, the language of his village. She was not surprised, as most of the children who came from

Kachin did not speak Burmese. If they have been able to attend village schools, they only know some Burmese. Sui Zi would need to tell the children's home that Mang Lian Hup only spoke Jingpho and would need tutoring in Burmese.

"Would you like to go to school?" Sui Zi asked him.

He replied, "Some of the kids I know go to school, and they only work at the farm when they are not at school. Maybe next year *A Phua* can send me to school too."

The village pastor then returned to drive Sui Zi back to the train station, and Mang Lian Hup asked if he could go back to playing with his friends. *A Phua* gave him permission so they could speak in private. Sui Zi and the pastor prayed with the *a phua* for God to guide her on the best decision for Mang Lian Hup's future and to give her peace with that decision. Sui Zi said, "I will call the home's pastor and tell him all I have learned about Mang Lian Hup. I will be in touch with the village pastor, and when you decide next week whether or not to send him, you can tell your pastor, and he will call me. If you agree to send him, he should try to be ready to leave in four weeks to be at the children's home for a few months before school starts."

Sui Zi believed Mang Lian Hup was the right age and had the right temperament for the home. He was a pleasant boy who showed intelligence beyond his years and would easily catch up to his school class. As a teacher, Sui Zi had experience and insight to make solid judgment calls on the children who could learn and do well in school. The children's homes wanted children they could educate, disciple, and send back to the community.

As the pastor drove Sui Zi back to the train station, he explained how their village church helped the *a phua* with rice and other items she needed for the boy. He said, "The role of the church is to care for widows and orphans in need, and our village church family is supporting this *a phua* and others with what God has given us. They are quick to give back what they can to their community in love and support."

Sui Zi said, "The church in Kachin State always reminds me of the early church in Acts as they bring all their resources together to help each other. Along with the church, my husband and I will be praying for *A Phua*, Mang Lian Hup, and the village church."

"Thank you. I pray for your safe travel back to Myitkyina and will be in touch about the *a phua*'s decision."

When the train arrived back in Myitkyina, Sui Zi stretched and climbed down the steps of the train, relieved to be home. As she walked out of the train station, she glanced through the row of cabs for her husband, Ja San. He sat in his green-and-white cab, ready to help her with her bag and drive back to their apartment.

They trudged up four flights of stairs to their two-room apartment. Ja San prepared tea while Sui Zi boiled chicken and steamed rice for their dinner. This seemed to be a tribute to the village children after Sui Zi had been in the village because it was a favorite of the children, whereas in the city they mostly fried their chicken.

After dinner, Sui Zi called the leader of Hope Christian Children's Home, Pastor Bawi, to tell him about Mang Lian Hup. Ja San listened as she told Pastor Bawi about Mang Lian Hup's background, alleviating his concerns about the child's age and no schooling. She said, "Based on my teaching experience, I witnessed an intelligent child who was engaged and eager to learn. He could easily catch up to Standard 2 in school. I know this home has several tuition teachers who could assist Mang Lian Hup in catching up."

After the discussion, Pastor Bawi agreed. "If Mang Lian Hup's *a phua* wants to send him, the boy could be placed in

Hope Christian Children's Home. We will all be in prayer for Mang Lian Hup and his *a phua*."

Sui Zi and Ja San ate their dinner and discussed Mang Lian Hup in more detail. Ja San said, "I love you and your heart for children, but you risk government prosecution when you work on behalf of the children in Chin and Kachin States by sending orphaned and impoverished children to Christian children's homes that you work with across Myanmar. I do want you to be safe."

Sui Zi worked as a Standard 3 teacher and gave tuition classes to earn extra money. She went to the refugee camp near their home every week where families lived who had been displaced by the civil war in Kachin State. Most of them did not speak Burmese and had trouble understanding the government officials' directions, so Sui Zi gave Burmese language lessons to the refugees. She believed it was her duty to translate, teach, and support the families in the camp and also to watch for orphans who came into the camp, so she could appeal to the Christian children's homes for assistance.

Two weeks passed quickly as Sui Zi taught tuition classes, visited the refugee camp, and prepared to teach Standard 3 in the new school year. Sui Zi, Ja San, and their church continued to pray for Mang Lian Hup's *a phua*'s decision. Finally, the village pastor called Sui Zi. "*A Phua* has tearfully agreed to send Mang Lian Hup to the children's home. We will be working with Mang Lian Hup to prepare him for Hope Christian Children's Home."

"Maybe I should make another visit before coming to take Mang Lian Hup to the children's home," Sui Zi suggested. The village pastor agreed, and they set the next Friday as the day for her visit.

These trips were expensive for Sui Zi and Ja San. They saved her money from teaching to pay for travel costs because sometimes the children's homes didn't have the funds to pay. Depending on which home the child was going to, a train or bus ticket and food were required for the trip for both Sui Zi and the child.

Sui Zi watched the mountains as the train traveled through Kachin State to the village where Mang Lian Hup lived. She prayed for the transition he and his *a phua* would go through over the next couple of weeks. It would be hard for *A Phua* emotionally to be a part of this even though she knew it was best for Mang Lian Hup. Sui Zi thought of her own grandchildren. She imagined how hard it would be to send one of them away to school, knowing she might never see them again. The train trip from Kachin State to the children's home was a long one, and Mang Lian Hup's *a phua* could be saying goodbye to Mang Lian Hup forever. Some children returned to their villages to be primary teachers after Standard 11. Others went on to the university to get degrees or to Bible college to become pastors. Many remained in the city to work near the children's home because they didn't have any remaining family.

The village pastor met Sui Zi at the train station and drove her back to the village. When she entered the village, *A Phua* and Mang Lian Hup were waiting. Mang Lian Hup looked sad and fearful; he hung his head and stared at the ground. Sui Zi approached him and greeted them in the name of Jesus as she silently prayed in her heart for God to give Mang Lian Hup peace with this decision. She entered their hut, accepted the tea, and told Mang Lian Hup about the children's home. "You will have good food to eat and clothes to wear; you will go to school and have tuition classes. More than twenty children live at Hope Christian Children's Home, so you will have many friends. Close to the home is a church where you will go with the other children on Sunday for Bible study and worship services."

"Will they teach me about King David?" Mang Lian Hup asked. "My favorite Bible story is David and Goliath."

"Yes, they will talk about King David. Also, I usually visit Hope Christian Children's Home several times a year. I will try to bring news from your *a phua* and take messages back from you also. The boys at the school love to play futball."

"Do they have a goalkeeper?" he asked, "because that is the position I like to play."

Sui Zi smiled and guaranteed him that he would get a turn to be the goalkeeper. After she answered more of Mang Lian Hup's questions, he seemed to be finished with the conversation, and his *a phua* told him to go out and play. "Is there any way I could accompany Mang Lian Hup to the children's home?" she asked.

"That would be very expensive. I'm sorry, but there are not enough funds." They discussed whether she could visit Mang Lian Hup.

A Phua asked, "Is there any way I can talk with Pastor Bawi at the children's home?"

Sui Zi pulled out her cell phone and called Pastor Bawi. She gave the phone to *A Phua* and left the hut to give *A Phua* some privacy.

Several minutes later, *A Phua* came out and said, "I am satisfied with Pastor Bawi's answers. He assured me he would raise Mang Lian Hup as his own son, and I can visit anytime I have the funds for the train ride. I am even welcome to stay with his family when I go. Best of all, he told me that he would make sure Mang Lian Hup always remembers me."

A Phua then said, "I will work hard to make extra strawberry baskets and save for the train ticket to visit Mang Lian Hup in one year." They discussed plans for Sui Zi to come back in two weeks, and together she and Mang Lian Hup would leave for the children's home on the next morning's train. As Sui Zi left the village, she saw Mang Lian Hup playing futball and waved goodbye to him. He hesitantly waved back. Sui Zi knew it was always hard on the children to leave the only family they had. In many ways it was easier with orphans, because they had no one; placing them in the children's home gave them a family. Due to the war in Kachin State, there were many orphans. Sui Zi continued to pray for Mang Lian Hup and his *a phua*.

The two weeks passed quickly, and Sui Zi returned to the train station that she seemed to have just left. She stood on the busy platform as Mang Lian Hup and his *a phua* said their goodbyes. Mang Lian Hup cried when his *a phua* promised him that, God willing, she would see him in a year. He held on to her tightly, and she said, "I love you, Mang Lian Hup."

Then *A Phua* pushed him back, reached into her pocket, and took out a necklace that was made with a flat, oval rock and a brown, wooden bead secured by tan, woven thread. She tied it around his neck. "Wear this all the time to remember me." She kissed him and then gave Sui Zi his hand. Sui Zi hugged *A Phua* and said goodbye to her and the village pastor.

Sui Zi quickly walked Mang Lian Hup onto the train and gave their tickets to the conductor. She did not have enough money for a sleeper car, so they traveled in the ordinary class on the passenger train. She did have money for food at station stops and had packed rice, vegetables, and boiled chicken in lunch tins for them too. She always tried to include the child's favorite food for the packed lunch.

Mang Lian Hup hung out the window and waved to his *a phua* from the yellow bench where she and the village pastor were seated. They were both in tears, so Sui Zi prayed for them as they waited for the train to leave. The village pastor had his arm around *A Phua* and supported her as best he could. This separation was the hardest part of the ministry. Sui Zi continued to pray to God that this would be a blessing not just for Mang Lian Hup but for his *a phua* as well.

As the train pulled away from the station, Mang Lian Hup waved until he could no longer see his *a phua*. Sui Zi sat quietly next to Mang Lian Hup as he cried. She knew he needed time, and it was best just to be there with him, praying. After a bit Mang Lian Hup stopped crying and watched out the window as the train rambled along the tracks. Sui Zi offered him water, which he took and drank. "Have you ever been on a train before?" she asked him.

He shook his head but then said, "My *a phua* told me about the train, how long the ride will be. She likes train rides and thinks I will like it too. She has traveled two times by train."

"Yes," Sui Zi said, " the ride will be long with many stops at different train stations as we travel to Mandalay where the Hope Christian Children's Home is located." As they talked, Sui Zi noticed he was looking around to take in the train. With such a full train, they could be thankful they had a bench by the window. As they traveled, Mang Lian Hup saw many new sights as they left the mountains and progressed across the country.

At the Napa train stop, Mang Lian Hup gazed hungrily at the vendors who walked by the train windows and down the train aisles selling food. Sui Zi asked Mang Lian Hup, "Are you ready to eat?" He quickly nodded. Sui Zi opened their lunch tins, and he devoured his boiled chicken, vegetables, and rice. He ate so fast Sui Zi realized how hungry he had been and offered him more from her lunch, which he also gobbled up. She had seen the small portions his *a phua* had fed him and realized he must have always been left hungry, especially as hard as he played and worked in the strawberry fields. After lunch, Sui Zi pointed out different sights as they traveled the railways to Mandalay.

After a while, Mang Lian Hup was engaged in his surroundings and even waved back at some children who ran along the train tracks when they passed through a village. He pointed out the houses built on stilts along the wetlands and numerous golden pagodas that dotted the skyline as they traveled.

At the next stop, they used the facilities at the train station, and Sui Zi surprised Mang Lian Hup. "Here is a bag of popcorn and a cup of ice cream." He had never had ice cream, and he was eating it so fast it made his head hurt. "Don't eat it so fast; enjoy it slowly," she told him.

At the next stop they bought bags of soup from one of the vendors for their dinner. Mang Lian Hup relaxed and became content with the travel. Several times he cozied up to Sui Zi and rested. He and Sui Zi slept occasionally as the long, overnight trip continued.

Exhausted from the hours of travel, Sui Zi and Mang Lian Hup finally arrived in Mandalay where they were greeted by a waving and smiling Pastor Bawi as soon as they exited the train station. With him was Hope Christian Children's Home manager, Seng Awn Lungjung, and their driver. Mang Lian Hup clung to Sui Zi as he was introduced to everyone. Pastor Bawi wore his usual white shirt and checkered *longyi*. He dressed in the traditional *longyi* for work and only wore casual clothes outside of work.

Pastor Bawi knelt down to be at eye level with Mang Lian Hup. "I am so glad to have you join my family." He patted him on the head. "Do you need anything before we start on the car ride to my apartment?" Mang Lian Hup shook his head, so they were off in the car to Pastor Bawi's home. This was Mang Lian Hup's second car ride, and Pastor Bawi showed him various sights along the way. The children's home was located in an apartment building, much like Sui Zi's own apartment. Pastor Bawi rented six apartments to house his family and the twenty children. Sui Zi planned to stay with them for three days to help

Mang Lian Hup adjust to his new life. During this time she could check in on the other children she had brought to the home.

Pastor Bawi's wife had lunch and tea ready for the weary travelers when they arrived, but first Pastor Bawi wanted Mang Lian Hup to meet the children who were flocking around to meet him. As he was introduced to the children, he stayed close to Sui Zi's side. One of the boys, Mai Jar, who was two years older than Mang Lian Hup, asked Sui Zi, "How are you doing?" Mai Jar was a child she had placed at the home with his older brother two years earlier.

"I am doing is fine. How are you doing and where is your brother?"

"He is in tuition class and doing very well. He is very happy to live here." Mai Jar then turned to Mang Lian Hup. "Do you play futball?"

Mang Lian Hup smiled. "Yes, and I am a goalie."

"I am also a goalie and love to play futball too. It will be good to have another good goalie. Would you like to sit with me for lunch?" He took Mang Lian Hup to the line to wait for their food.

Mang Lian Hup's eyes grew wide when he saw his large servings of rice, vegetables, and beef. "Do you always eat this good?"

"Yes, the food is always very good."

Sui Zi backed away and joined Pastor Bawi, his wife, and Seng Awn Lungjung for the meal. As they ate lunch and drank tea, Sui Zi filled them in on the details of Mang Lian Hup's story. Seng Awn Lungjung planned to begin tutoring him immediately to get him ready for school. They glanced over at Mang Lian Hup as he ate. "I am so pleased," Pastor Bawi began, "that Mai Jar is helping our new resident and talking with him. Mai Jar is also from Kachin State and speaks the same dialect as Mang Lian Hup. I had asked Mai Jar specifically to befriend and help

Mang Lian Hup. I'm always pleased to see the children work hard to help each other, especially when they first arrive."

With Mang Lian Hup settled in, Sui Zi asked about the building of the new children's home. Pastor Bawi explained, "I am still trying to secure funds by working with the churches in Singapore to raise money for the new home." He had been able to purchase nearby land with the help of several Mandalay Christian churches that supported Hope Christian Children's Home. Sui Zi and Pastor Bawi walked to that land every time she came and prayed over it for both the funds to build the home and for more sponsors to support the children. He worked hard for the funds and support for the twenty children he was currently raising. Encouraged by the progress of the new building, Sui Zi hoped to bring more children to experience new beginnings.

When they returned to the apartments, the children had finished eating, and some were headed to tuition classes while others went outside to play in the street or in the different apartment rooms. Pastor Bawi and Sui Zi found Mai Jar and Mang Lian Hup talking and playing marbles together. Mang Lian Hup looked up. When he saw Pastor Bawi and Sui Zi watching them, he smiled from ear to ear. Pastor Bawi told Sui Zi that she was right: Mang Lian Hup had a great smile.

Pastor Bawi asked Mang Lian Hup if he would like to clean up and get some new clothes. They showed him where the shower was and gave him a bar of soap, washcloths, towels, toothpaste, toothbrush, comb, underwear, an outfit for school, and a couple of outfits for play, along with a pair of sandals. Mang Lian Hup had never been given so many new things, but he shyly accepted each one. He had to be shown how the shower worked because he had only bathed in the stream or with water in a barrel his *a phua* used.

Then they showed him the mat where he would sleep next to Mai Jar and where to store his belongings. After he was all cleaned up and dressed, Pastor Bawi gathered his flock of children together for their weekly allowance. He explained to Mang Lian Hup, "This money is for the chores the children do as they help care for the home during the week. It can be saved or used as they like. During school time, however, it has to be saved until the end of the week in case the teacher asks them to buy supplies. If they have money left over at the end of the week, they are free to spend it in the local market."

Since school was not in session, the children gathered to walk to the local shops. They strolled along until they reached the land where the new home would be built. They stopped to pray for the funds to finish the building. Then they continued on the narrow pathways that were lined with tin-roofed shanties that served as both homes and storefronts. The wood-framed canopies contained many household items as well as toys, snacks, and sweets. They stopped at the different huts that the children frequented to buy things.

Sui Zi and Pastor Bawi walked along with Mai Jar and Mang Lian Hup and listened to the boys talk about buying new marbles and rubber bands to play with. The boys examined cookies, spicy chips, and hard candy. Mai Jar and Mang Lian Hup each bought a bag of rubber bands, some marbles, cookies, and some spicy snacks. Once they were back at the home, Mai Jar and a group of boys showed Mang Lian Hup how to play rubber bands. They each snapped a rubber band into the air; the boy who snapped his rubber band on top of the others won them all. Determining which rubber band was the most on top to designate the winner led to much discussion.

The boys played this game with lots of laughs and smiles. Sui Zi smiled at how quickly Mang Lian Hup warmed up to the other boys. She was happy to hear Pastor Bawi and Seng Awn Lungjung speak to Mang Lian Hup first in Burmese and then translate to Jingpho. They wanted to immerse him in Burmese to help him quickly learn the language.

As the children put their new treasures in their footlockers, dinner was called. They were treated to a flavorful dinner of rice, vegetables, chickpeas with dahl, and large slices of watermelon for dessert. Mang Lian Hup stayed close to Mai Jar and laughed at some of the things Mai Jar said to him. By the time they were done with dinner, not a speck of food remained on the boys' plates.

After dinner the boys burned off some energy in a futball game with some of the children who lived in the apartment building. Mang Lian Hup was thrilled to play and show his skills. A rigorous futball match provided great enjoyment for the boys.

After playtime the children headed to do their chores or attend tuition classes. Mang Lian Hup tagged along with Mai Jar to his tuition class. As Mai Jar studied his subjects, Seng Awn Lungjung sat with Mang Lian Hup and helped him learn Burmese. Even though Sui Zi was tired from two days of travel, she stayed and helped with the tuition classes for a chance to see the children learn.

When it was time for bed, Mang Lian Hup settled on his mat. Sui Zi joined Pastor Bawi and his wife for a few minutes before she retired to a room. She shared a room with some of the girls who lived in one of the six apartments. Sui Zi quietly got ready for bed so she wouldn't disturb the girls who were already asleep. She prayed for Mang Lian Hup and his *a phua*, the children at the home, and the funds for the new home. She thanked God for their safe travel and that Mang Lian Hup appeared to be adjusting well. She had not expected him to adjust so quickly after the tearful goodbye with his *a phua*. She had noticed that occasionally she saw him holding the stone on his necklace and rubbing it between his fingers. She wondered if he thought of his *a phua* at those moments. Sui Zi was grateful that Mai Jar helped Mang Lian Hup and acted like a big brother to him. She prayed that they would become great friends. Overall, it was going well, and with a grateful heart Sui Zi settled exhausted into sleep.

Time passed quickly at the children's home with all the activities that the children had going on. Soon it was Sunday, and they all walked to the church, which was located next to the land that had been purchased for the new home. Sui Zi wondered how Mang Lian Hup would do since he did not know the language. She saw him sit through children's Bible study and church while Mai Jar quietly translated for him. He recognized some of the songs and sang along in his native Jingpho language. He had an angelic, peaceful face as he sang during worship.

"Mang Lian Hup's *a phua* has raised him well to know and worship God," Pastor Bawi told Sui Zi. After church, she visited with Mai Jar and his older half brother, Ram Tha Hmung. They asked her, "Have you seen our *mi khin*?"

"Due to increased military fighting, I rarely get up to the part of Kachin State where your *mi khin* lives. Many people in that area of Kachin State are now displaced by the war," Sui Zi explained to them.

"We have not heard news of her in the last two years since we came to the children's home," they said.

Sui Zi said, "I will contact the pastors in your *mi khin*'s area of Kachin State to see if I can get an update on her. If I am able to get any information, I will let you know. It is common for people in the war-stricken areas to move frequently."

"If you speak with *Mi Khin*," Ram Tha Hmung said, "please tell her we are fine and happy living in the children's home. And tell her I am looking out for Mai Jar. We are both doing very well in school." It was so good to see how both of these boys were thriving two years after their placement.

"I will certainly share your news. I am so happy to hear that you are doing well and helping each other." Ram Tha Hmung and Sui Zi discussed his plans to go to the university to study engineering when he passed his exams. "Mai Jar, what are your plans for your future education?" Sui Zi asked.

Mai Jar quickly responded, "I am going to study mathematics when I get to the university because I would like to be a trader of goods."

"What goods would you like to trade?"

"I think food goods like mustard and cabbage."

Sui Zi was pleased. "Thank you, Mai Jar, for being a helper with Mang Lian Hup. Will you look after Mang Lian Hup like Ram Tha Hmung looks after you?"

Mai Jar smiled and promised he would look after Mang Lian Hup like a younger brother.

Monday morning it was time for Sui Zi to head back to Myitkyina. Mang Lian Hup stood with Pastor Bawi's arm around him and waited to say goodbye to Sui Zi. He had already taken to Pastor Bawi and looked up to him like a *phan khin* (father).

"I must go back home, but I'll be back to see you very soon," Sui Zi told Mang Lian Hup. "Do you have a message that I can take back to your *a phua*?"

He said, "Tell *A Phua* I am very well, think of her often, and for her to please come visit when she can, so she can have good food too."

Sui Zi assured him she would tell his *a phua* and gave him a hug before leaving for the train station.

Mai Jar

Sui Zi thought about Mai Jar and Ram Tha Hmung as she waited for the train to arrive that would take her from Mandalay back to Myitkyina. Two years was a long time for them to be separated from their mother with no communication. The boys were doing well, and she praised God for this because they had had a rough life before coming to Hope Christian Children's Home. The trip to rescue them had been dangerous but was coordinated by several pastors.

Mai Jar and his brother, Ram Tha Hmung, had progressed over that time, and they both looked healthy and vibrant now.

They had gained weight, and their eyes were white and bright. To see them laugh and play with each other and other children brought pleasure to her. They had adapted well to the children's home, and she praised God for Pastor Bawi and the work he was doing on behalf of Christian orphans in Myanmar.

Sui Zi boarded the train and took a seat on a yellow bench by a window. She settled in to rest during the train ride home and reminisced about her trip two years ago to rescue those two boys, Mai Jar and Ram Tha Hmung, in the northern part of Kachin State, past Putao near the Chinese border.

Sui Zi had traveled by bus and then by car with the pastor who had met her at the bus stop. As they drove, they discussed the KIA efforts in the area against the Tatmadaw. "Fighting has been intense, and Mai Jar's *phan khin*, Bai Za Thawng, had been a soldier for the KIA," the pastor had told her. "He was killed in a battle against the Tatmadaw a year earlier. Intense fighting drove their mother away from the village where they lived after her husband's death. Her two boys were in poor health, and the mother could not provide for them, herself, and their elderly grandparents who were with her. The boys had been out of school for a year because their mother couldn't make enough money to send them to school."

Sui Zi recalled that they drove into a small village, and she noticed a group of boys playing futball with a homemade futball. She saw boys do this in many villages. When fruit was in season, the boys used green grapefruits as futballs. At other times when fruit was not in season, they would take a rock and tie old clothes around it to soften it for kicking. These boys played barefoot and had a great time with their homemade futball.

Sui Zi had wondered if any of these boys were the ones she was there to meet. She had seen the makeshift village of pole tents and fires and the cleared area where they grew mustard. The pastor and Sui Zi found Mai Jar and his *mih khin*, Hnem

Sung, where she worked to harvest mustard greens. Mai Jar also worked; he took the baskets of greens and sorted out the good ones from the bad ones. The pastor brought lunch for the family because they were interrupting the workday. He knew food was scarce for this family, so he had provided boiled chicken, rice, and vegetable curry.

Sui Zi remembered that Mai Jar was very small and thin for a seven-year-old boy. His bones stretched his skin to sharp ridges and points, and his tired eyes were yellow and dull. He avoided looking at Sui Zi and stayed close to his *mih khin*'s side. When his brother, Ram Tha Hmung, joined them, she recalled that he was also thin for his twelve years, but he had been one of the boys playing futball when they entered the village. Ram Tha Hmung's eyes were also yellow and tired looking. Mai Jar's *mih khin* put a kettle of water on to warm for tea with their lunch. "We have been up since dawn, working in the fields; Ram Tha Hmung has just had a play break. Thank you, Pastor, for bringing them lunch. Things are very hard for us, and we only have one meal a day."

Then she introduced them to Mai Jar and Ram Tha Hmung's grandparents who also lived with them. Due to their age, they did not work much but helped as best they could.

"Is your work in the mustard field your only source of income?" Sui Zi had asked.

"Oh, I also do wash in the evenings for more money."

Sui Zi could still picture the pastor as he blessed the meal before they settled in for lunch. Ram Tha Hmung ravenously ate his food, whereas Mai Jar seemed overwhelmed. "There is so much food and it is very good."

The whole family enjoyed the meal, and when it was done, the *a phua* said, "I will clean up the dishes while *A Bo* and Ram Tha Hmung go back to work."

Mai Jar replied, "I don't want to go back; I want to stay with Mother."

Sui Zi had been touched when his mother gently said, "Mai Jar, it is time for work. I will join you after I talk with Sui Zi and Pastor. You go with Ram Tha Hmung and sort what you picked this afternoon." She sighed as Mai Jar went off with Ram Tha Hmung and his *a bo*. She then turned to us with tears in her eyes, silent and struggling with what to say. "Thank you again, Pastor, for the food. Before my husband was killed, we had plenty of food and a good life."

"Please tell us about your life before your husband was killed," Sui Zi remembered saying.

"Oh, times were much better then. We lived in a village near a large river with plenty of fish. Together we worked in the fields. Sometimes Bai Za Thawng (her husband) also worked to find jewels for extra money. He thought Mai Jar was the lucky one because one time he took him along and found a nice gem that brought in good money." Hnem Sung smiled at the memory.

"My husband was also a reserve soldier in the KIA. I didn't worry about marrying him because there had been a sixteen-year-long cease-fire in place between the KIA and the Tatmadaw. He went for drills when called, but all in all it was just a good life. We had lived in a two-room shack with his parents who slept in the cooking room; our family slept together in the other room. I had no other family and enjoyed having his parents around too.

"I was thankful to find a Christian man who wanted to marry me even though I had a four-year-old child. My first husband had abandoned me when Ram Tha Hmung was two, so I was grateful to have a new husband who was a good Christian man and a father for Ram Tha Hmung.

"Mai Jar was born in our first year of marriage, and his father was very proud to have a son. We attended the village church three miles from the village where the boys went to school. We all worked hard and had plenty of food and money to send Ram Tha Hmung to school when he was old enough. We always had three meals a day and meat several times a week.

"But when Mai Jar was two, the Tatmadaw broke the cease-fire and attacked the KIA. Bai Za Thawng was called up to active duty with the renewed fighting. He was very much against the Myanmar military rule. He believed that the Myanmar government that broke the cease-fire agreement had to be stopped. His unit would go out for a while and then return on leave. Things got harder for us because he no longer worked the farm. The grandparents and I did our best to continue, and Ram Tha Hmung was still able to attend school.

"Two years into the renewed war, the fight came near our village; I worried about our safety. Then I got word that Bai Za Thawng had died in a battle. Mai Jar was four years old when his father was killed. We stayed in the village for another year, but the battles came closer and closer. I could hear the *pop-pop-pop* of gunfire. Many villagers planned to leave, so we decided to pack what we could and go with them.

"We carried whatever we could and left our home in the village. We headed southwest and made tent-like pole shelters because the refugees would stop to rest. We finally ended up near Putao in our current village. Ram Tha Hmung and his *a bo* worked to make the shelter that we live in now, which is a sturdy one-room pole tent. We started working in the mustard fields to earn money. I take the harvest to market in Putao when it is ready and do wash to help support the family. The grandparents do not work as much as they used to because they are elderly.

"I can no longer afford to send my children to school. Ram Tha Hmung only made it to Class 4, and Mai Jar has not attended school yet. I'm worried that they are not getting enough food to grow and be healthy. I miss my husband and the life we had before the fighting started back up."

Sui Zi recalled that she told her about Hope Christian Children's Home and Pastor Bawi. "The boys will have three meals a day plus snacks, go to school, and attend tuition classes. Pastor Bawi gives the children clothes and insists they be well groomed. They are provided with healthcare, but most importantly, Pastor Bawi will raise them as Christians with the vision that they either become primary class teachers or attend the university or Bible college, based on the children's desires and grades. The children's home is a happy place and growing. Many staff members are dedicated to caring for the children."

Hnem Sung had looked at her with yearning in her eyes. "I only want to give my sons hope and a future from God's Word."

The memory was so vivid Sui Zi could almost feel her hand as she took it and said, "I believe God has sent me to fulfill that promise for you. Do the boys know that you are thinking of sending them to the children's home?"

Hnem Sung shook her head. "I wanted to meet you and hear about the home first. I know this probably means I will never see them again, and I'm not sure how to tell them they are going away. I think that between me and *A Bo*, we can take care of the three of us, but it will be better for my sons to go. However, it hurts especially to let Mai Jar go. He rarely leaves my side, even to play futball."

"I can see understanding and intelligence in Ram Tha Hmung, and he will help Mai Jar make this move easier," Sui Zi had told her. "Pastor Bawi will embrace the boys as sons and care for them as his own. It amazes me how Pastor Bawi can care so well for the twenty-plus children consistently in his care."

Reluctantly Hnem Sung agreed to let the boys go with Sui Zi in one month. "I will tell the boys and give them time to adjust. My biggest concern is how they will find me again. With the fighting moving closer, we know we will probably end up moving again."

"We will do our best to stay in touch with you. I will let Sui Zi know where the boys are going," the pastor had reassured her. They agreed that he would be with the boys part of the way on their journey to Hope Christian Children's Home by taking them to Sui Zi at the bus stop.

Sui Zi then said, "I will pray for you and the boys during this transition. God willing, we will find a way to be together again, and after the boys are educated, they should be able to care for you in your older years."

One month later Sui Zi had arrived at the bus station in Putao and found the pastor, Ram Tha Hmung, and Mai Jar waiting for her. She waved as the bus pulled in and got her things ready to exit the bus. She walked straight to them and greeted each boy with a gentle hug and warm smile. She noticed their clothes had been laundered and they were much cleaner than when she had seen them before. "You look very handsome," she had told the boys.

"Our mother insisted we bathe for the trip and wear our best clothes," Ram Tha Hmung responded.

They had time before the bus left for Myitkyina where they would spend the night before their train ride to Mandalay. "Maybe we should find some lunch," Sui Zi remembered suggesting to the pastor. They walked into the city and found a street vendor with small tables and plastic chairs. They sat down and ordered a rice-and-vegetable curry. The boys watched everything around them as the market was full and busy.

The pastor had told her that the boys were doing quite well. Mai Jar had cried a while, and Ram Tha Hmung had comforted him. "The church took an offering to help with the cost of the trip to Mandalay for the boys."

"My church has also taken a collection for them. There is

plenty to treat the boys to meals and snacks as they travel on this long journey. How did their mother and grandparents handle the boys leaving?"

"Not too well – even knowing it was for the best."

She nodded in understanding and said, "I will pray for them."

The memory of their lunch stirred compassion in Sui Zi's heart. Ram Tha Hmung had quickly finished eating while Mai Jar picked at his food and watched all the sights in the market. Then they all walked back to the bus station.

"We will take a bus to my home in Myitkyina," Sui Zi told them, "and spend the night at my house. In the morning we board the train for Mandalay. You will be able to see many different sights from the train."

Ram Tha Hmung had talked openly with Sui Zi while Mai Jar hung on quietly to Ram Tha Hmung. The pastor stayed with them until it was time to board the bus. He prayed over them for travel safety and for the boys as they journeyed to Hope Christian Children's Home.

Sui Zi recalled her own doubts as she settled the three of them on the bus. She wondered if these boys would have done better in the Grace Christian Children's Home. It was a rural home and not in a busy city, but at this time they did not have any openings. It would be something to remember if the boys had any trouble at Hope.

The bus ride had been uneventful, and Mai Jar slept on his brother's lap for much of the trip. Ja San, Sui Zi's husband, met them at the bus station, and they rode in his taxi to the apartment building. They all went upstairs to the small apartment. "Please make yourselves at home, and we will prepare dinner," Sui Zi told them.

Ja San quickly engaged the boys in a discussion of futball. "At the children's home you will be able to play futball with other boys." He also asked them about the bus ride while Sui Zi boiled chicken, vegetables, and rice for dinner. Sui Zi remembered the sweet moments when they sat down for dinner, prayed over the meal, and gave thanks for safe travel that day. Sui Zi had noticed that Mai Jar finished all of his food, which pleased her, since he had not eaten much at lunch and had refused snacks on the bus ride. As she did the dishes, her husband took the boys out for a walk to stretch and get some exercise.

Then she recalled her worry when they had been gone for over an hour. She was going to go out and look for them when she heard them coming up the stairs. The boys were excited from playing futball with a brand-new ball her husband had purchased for them on their walk. He just smiled at her when she gently shook her head at him. He always gave the children who spent the night with them some little item from the toy store down the street.

That night they sat down and talked with the boys. Somehow the discussion of Christmas came up, and the boys eagerly talked about their memories of Christmas. "The whole village saves throughout the year to have a pig roast on Christmas Day," Ram Tha Hmung said. "I help our stepfather hang decorations around the church for Christmas. We take vines and flowers that we've gathered in the woods and decorate the poles of the building. Mai Jar and I would go caroling on Christmas Eve, singing songs in exchange for little gifts. We'd get a handful of rice, corn, fruit, or other small gifts. My favorite carol is 'Silent Night.'

"On Christmas Day everyone goes to church, wearing their new Christmas clothes. We each got a new white shirt and gum for Christmas. I can make one piece of gum last a whole week. I would hide it in the shack, but sometimes my gum disappeared, and I'd yell, 'Who took my gum?' After church the whole village would gather to eat the pig that had been roasting. Everyone was to bring a dish to share."

Mai Jar said, "We had a lot of rice dishes with the pig."

"But," Ram Tha Hmung had added, "we have not had a good Christmas celebration since our stepfather died."

"You will have a nice Christmas again at the children's home," Sui Zi told them. "Pastor Bawi enjoys celebrating the holidays with the children."

The boys lay down on mats that Sui Zi put down for them, and she and her husband went to sleep in the other room. When Sui Zi went out to check on them, she saw that Mai Jar had rolled off his mat and into his brother and was snuggled up tight with him. She re-covered both boys with their blankets and then went back to her bed.

The next morning Sui Zi and Ja San were up before the boys. They had prayed for the upcoming trip, for the boys to adjust well at Hope, and for their *mih khin, a phua,* and *a bo* to have peace with this tough decision.

Sui Zi had combed her long, black hair and put on traveling clothes. She got her *kyauk pyin* (grinding stone) out and ground the *thanaka*, then she added some water to make a creamy paste. She applied the thanaka cream in round, yellow circles on her cheeks. Then she was ready. She woke the boys and prepared their breakfast, which was simply rice and vegetable curry. The boys gathered their small bundles of clothes and the futball that they had been given when it was time to head to the train station.

The train was an hour late that day, so they had a long wait at the station. The boys had played with their new futball and watched the trains. They had never seen a train before, and this led to much discussion about the tracks and how the train works. Ram Tha Hmung liked to hear the whistle on the trains. Sui Zi bought them some snacks, and Mai Jar even smiled, which warmed her heart.

When their train arrived, they climbed aboard and found

a yellow bench to sit on where all three of them could squeeze side by side. The boys had been very excited to get on board and feel the train move, but about a half hour later, Mai Jar said his stomach hurt. His forehead was sweaty, so Sui Zi had him sit next to the window to get some fresh air. Before too long, the motion sickness got the better of him and he threw up. Ram Tha Hmung helped clean Mai Jar up and care for him. They got off the train at the stops, but the motion sickness plagued Mai Jar the entire train ride. Sui Zi had worried because Mai Jar was small, and she didn't want him to dehydrate, but every time he drank or ate, it came right back up. When they arrived in Mandalay, they had a very tired and sick little boy.

Pastor Bawi had smiled and waved to them as the train pulled into the station like he always did. Sui Zi gathered Mai Jar into her arms to carry him off the train. Ram Tha Hmung carried all of their other things. Pastor Bawi quickly took Mai Jar and rushed to get him home to see what they could do to help him. Instead of stopping to introduce the boys to the rest of the children who were waiting to meet them, he took them straight into his apartment where his wife and mother-in-law could help discern if Mai Jar needed medical attention. Everyone had agreed it was motion sickness brought on by his first train ride and possibly made worse by eating larger portions of food than Mai Jar was used to having.

The memory of poor sick Mai Jar almost brought tears to Sui Zi's eyes. He had slowly sipped tea with extra sugar, and Ram Tha Hmung stayed close to him. Sui Zi explained how much Ram Tha Hmung had helped with Mai Jar on the train ride. Pastor Bawi praised him. "You are an excellent big brother. Let me take you to meet the other children." Soon Mai Jar was resting, and Ram Tha Hmung was getting to know the rest of the "family."

Sui Zi had said goodbye to the children and Pastor Bawi.

On the trip home, she thought about how Mai Jar had fully recovered. He still stayed close to Ram Tha Hmung, but Pastor Bawi said, "That will change as the boys start tuition classes and ease into the schedules for their age groups. Mai Jar and Ram Tha Hmung will be in the same room together, but since they are five years apart, their class schedules will be different."

Mai Jar had been playing with other children and eating with no problem by the time Sui Zi left. Sui Zi felt like she was the keeper of these children's stories and considered it a blessing that God would let her play a role in the rescue of orphaned Christians to help provide them with hope and a future. Sui Zi was pleased and contented to have seen how well these boys were doing after a difficult beginning. With all the reminiscing and memories of Mai Jar, the time on the train had flown by.

Then she prayed that God would bring a girl to the home. Hope Christian Children's Home had an opening because one of their girls was going to the university.

Mala

After contacting the pastors she worked with, Sui Zi decided that she would go to the refugee camp where she taught Burmese language classes to the children to see if any of the girls would be interested in moving to a children's home. She walked to the Mali Yang IDP (Internally Displaced Persons) refugee camp where the people live in government-established buildings. These long buildings have metal roofs and bamboo room dividers that separate the small living quarters. Without help from Christian organizations like the KBC (Kachin Baptist

Convention), the people who live in IDP refugee camps would be without food and basic medicine.

Sui Zi didn't think there was a durable solution to help the displaced people in Kachin State. She hoped that peace talks would bring about a cease-fire, but even then the people would need supplies to rebuild their villages and farms. The Tatmadaw would have to move from the area, and the land mines they put throughout the war zones would have to be removed. Sui Zi believed there would be no justice for the people of Kachin State until it was recognized as a state and a local state leader was established. It would be a long time before this could be achieved, and many of the children had already been in the refugee camp for several years.

Sui Zi reached the camp, and the children and some adults gathered around to practice their Burmese language. Most of the refugees spoke local dialects rather than Burmese, which made it difficult when the government officials met with them. So Sui Zi and some of the other teachers worked with them to help them understand basic Burmese language so they could communicate better.

On this day Sui Zi started by telling them about Hope Christian Children's Home. "The home has an opening for one girl. The girl would be well cared for and receive an education. Plans are being made for a new building that will be built for housing the children. If any of you are interested or know of a girl in need of help who wants to finish her education, would you please let me know?"

At the end of the class, one of the fourteen-year-old girls stayed to talk with Sui Zi. Mala was a bright young girl who often attended Sui Zi's class. "I was in Standard 8 before I came to the refugee camp and would be interested in finishing my education."

"What about your family? Where are they?" Sui Zi asked.

"I am the oldest in the family with three younger brothers and one younger sister. Both of my parents are still alive."

"We should make some time over the next couple of weeks to talk about this decision," Sui Zi suggested. "I will also need to talk with your parents about your request."

Mala looked hopeful at the thought of leaving the refugee camp and finishing her education. They walked together to meet Mala's parents. Sui Zi asked, "Mala, what do you want to do when you finish your education?"

Mala quickly answered, "I want to attend the university and study to be an accountant." That surprised Sui Zi because not many farm children in Kachin State would say that they wanted to be an accountant. But Mala continued. "One of my teachers told me that I would be good as an accountant since I am good with numbers."

They walked to the middle of one of the long buildings. Mala lived with her six other family members behind a plastic curtain in the small room. "My uncle and aunt live in the room next to ours with their five children," Mala explained.

"Hello," Sui Zi began. "I am Sui Zi, I teach Burmese language skills here at the camp, and I help the Christian children's homes. During class, I told of an opening for a girl at one of the homes. Your Mala came forward and asked about filling that opening. She would like the opportunity to finish her education."

"But why do we have to send her away? Can't you help the refugee children go to school here?" Mala's parents asked.

Sui Zi explained, "The refugees must live by the rules the government establishes for them, and schooling is not provided."

"We understand, but we would also like our five-year-old son to have at least a primary education. The other children have enough or have no desire for continuing education like Mala."

As they talked about the hardships of life in the refugee camp, sadness filled Sui Zi's heart that people had to live in such poverty. She could offer little hope outside of prayer. Mala's parents were Christians and Sui Zi told them that she would be in prayer with them over the decision on whether to send Mala away.

The next week Sui Zi and Mala spent time together, and Sui Zi told her more about the home and Pastor Bawi. "Pastor Bawi will welcome you to the children's home. He also said to tell your family that any of your brothers or your sister would be welcome to join you in one year because most of the funds for the new building have been provided. Your family was approved because of the hardship created by the war. God blessed the children's home with funds from a Singapore NGO (non-government organization). Pastor Bawi is working with Christian churches across Myanmar to raise the remaining twenty percent."

"My parents do not want the other children to go to school because they only need a primary education. They are needed to work the farm when they leave the refugee camp. My brothers and sister only want to be farmers like my parents. My younger sister does not like school and prefers to be at home with Mother."

"Tell me about your farm. What was life like when you lived there?" Sui Zi asked.

"We were very blessed. My parents had a large farm and produced many crops. They grew rice, beans, potatoes, and pumpkins. The whole family worked hard, and we did not move around; we stayed on the land they owned and farmed. I walked several miles every day to school. Before and after school, I would either help on the farm or do chores in the house. We lived in a four-room house my dad had built, which was much different from the cramped one-room space we have in the refugee camp. We had plenty of food at home, but here we are hungry."

"Did you have a church that you attended?" Sui Zi wanted to know more.

"Oh yes. When we lived on the farm at my parents' home, I went to church every Sunday. Singing and Sunday school were some of my favorite things in church. I love going to church. That is what I miss the most here in the refugee camp. I miss our village church."

"And what was your school like in your village?" Sui Zi recognized that Mala enjoyed telling her about the home she lost.

"In the village where we lived, there was only a primary school, and when I finished, I asked my parents to find a way for me to continue to go to school. I desired very much to finish my education. After much discussion, they decided to send me to my uncle's farm to live. He was my father's brother and lived a full day's walk from home, but there was a secondary school where I could go for seventh through eleventh standard. So they arranged for me to live with my uncle and aunt.

"I came home on school breaks to live with my family, but the rest of the year I went away for school. I was very excited to continue school and thought I would enjoy being with my cousins."

Mala's uncle and aunt had five children of their own. Mala's determination to get her education impressed Sui Zi. "You are very brave to move away from your family at such a young age to continue school."

Mala's eyes showed her sadness, so Sui Zi asked, "Was it hard to be away from your family?"

"I missed my family, but I thought this was what I had do if I didn't want to be a farmer."

"What was your life like with your uncle's family?"

"It was difficult. My aunt expected me to work very hard in exchange for my food and room. I was also expected to get good grades to prove to my parents that I was working hard at school. My aunt is a difficult woman to please, and she expected me to work on their farm, cook all the family's meals, and help with other household chores. I had to cook eight cups of rice in the morning and evening because they had great hunger.

"In my free time I was expected to study because there was no time to rest in my aunt's house. The absolute worst part was that I was not allowed to go with the family to church. I had to stay home and cook the family's meal and complete chores.

"For the year that I lived with them, I felt sorry for myself. I thought I had to work hard until I finished Standard 11 to acquire a better life, so I forced myself to work hard."

"Why didn't you tell your parents about the hardships with your uncle and aunt?"

"I thought it was my burden or trial, and that if I complained, I'd be sent home, and my education would stop."

"How did you get through these hard times?" Sui Zi asked.

"Singing worship songs helped me through those hardships. I also looked forward to break when I went home to my family," Mala answered.

"I am very impressed that such a young girl as you were would work so hard for her education," Sui Zi praised her.

Mala responded, "I prayed that someday I could go to the university and study accounting."

Sui Zi asked, "How did you come to live here in the refugee camp?"

Mala explained, "The fighting moved close to my uncle's village, and they made the decision to leave and go to my parents' home. We traveled a whole day with what we could carry from his home to my parents'. When we arrived, my uncle told them that the Tatmadaw were moving in that direction. The village down from theirs had been burned, and there was intensified fighting between the KIA and the Tatmadaw.

"My father was very concerned. He said they would have

to keep a close watch on what was happening and make plans for getting out if the fighting continued towards their village. Much discussion took place on where to go if we had to leave, and they decided to go to the capital. My father and uncle hoped to find work there in the city. Until then, my father had worked on my grandparents' farm. Even though the fighting drove us from my uncle's farm, it was good to be home and back in our church again."

"How did you end up coming to the refugee camp if you were headed to the capital?" Sui Zi inquired.

"The fighting came closer to our village. We heard the *pop-pop-pop* sound of the guns. My father heard that the village down from ours had been burned by the Tatmadaw, and we needed to leave. I had only been back home for a month. We again packed what we could carry on our backs. Father also packed some produce and items on a cart that made it look like we were going to the capital to sell produce. We left most of our belongings back in our home. He told us to be quiet when we got to the KIA lines and let him do the talking. We needed the KIA to let us cross their line in order to head to Myitkyina. We walked for days; I am not sure how long, but we camped at night and walked during the day. I was so scared for our safety that everything had become a blur. I think we walked for several days.

"When we came to the KIA main line, Father met with the sergeant, but they did not want us to pass. My father talked a long time with the sergeant and told him we needed to go to the capital to sell our produce and get more supplies for the next season. Finally, the sergeant in the KIA army let us pass the line with a promise from Father that we would quickly return. Father told us that the KIA wanted the villagers to stay and fight with them against the Tatmadaw. They wanted us to protect our villages and farms, or the government would seize our lands. I felt bad for my father; he had worked hard to build a nice home and farm. We did not know what would happen to the home and farm while we were gone. We kept traveling and praying for God's protection until we reached the city.

"I remember as we got closer to the city, we joined with other groups of people who were fleeing the war zones in their region. Once in the capital, the government directed the people to the refugee camps. They told us that the capital was full of refugees trying to escape the fighting. There was no work, and we should go to the refugee camp where they could care for us until the war was over. Then we could return to our villages.

"We came here eight months ago, and there is little hope of going back. The fighting seems to continue. We do not have enough food here, and we depend on the NGOs for food and clothes. To have no work or way to better our lives is not good for people. The government came one day and made a big show and took pictures of giving property and money to some of the families so they could leave the refugee camp. After the pictures were done, they took back what they had given, and the families still live here in the camp. The children's home and school is my way out, and maybe after I have an education I can move my family out of this camp also."

"Where would you move your family to?"

Mala responded, "If I am an accountant in a large city, I would move them to live with me."

As Sui Zi walked home from the refugee camp, she thought about how Mala seemed much older than her fourteen years. She was so mature it was like Sui Zi was talking with her own twenty-four-year-old daughter. Sui Zi determined to pray for Mala and her parents about this decision. She would want to take Mala in two weeks if they decided to send her. After that, the school year would be starting, and Sui Zi would be unable to take any more trips to the children's homes until the next break.

She decided to go back to the refugee camp and have another discussion with Mala's parents because Mala felt strongly that her nine-year-old brother should also go and finish his primary education. She was closest to this brother and had told Sui Zi he was a very good student and needed an education.

Sui Zi knew the parents wanted the boys to become farmers and help with their farm. She thought about the importance of education for the future of Myanmar. Many people in the villages thought a primary education was sufficient for their children – that basic math, writing, and reading were all a person needed. Sui Zi believed much more was needed for the children to be successful even in farming.

Two days later Sui Zi once again sat with Mala's family having tea. Her father said, "We have decided to send Mala to Hope Christian Children's Home, but I am concerned that Mala will be so far away. I am trusting Jesus to care for my child."

Sui Zi took this opportunity to tell Mala's father more about Pastor Bawi. "He is kind to the children, and they call him Papa. He takes care of each child as if they were his own. Pastor Bawi's wife, mother-in-law, and the home's director, Seng Awn Lungjung, all act like mothers to the children. Pastor Bawi will pair Mala with another girl close to her age to be her friend and help her adjust to the new home. In one year the children's home will be expanding and perhaps one of Mala's siblings could join her. I understand the desire to have the children become farmers with the family, but as long as they are in the refugee camp, it would be good for at least Mala's younger brother Lasa to join her and finish his primary education. Then, after a year, Mala would have family with her. You do not need to make a decision on Lasa until much later; please pray about it over the next year."

Twelve days later Sui Zi stood in the doorway of their room and waited for Mala to say her goodbyes. She hugged her mother, brothers, and sister goodbye. She thanked her father and told him she would work hard in school and make him proud. She took the bundle of her belongings she had packed to take with her, and they turned and walked to the end of the refugee camp where they got into Ja San's cab. He drove them to the railway station for the trip to Myitkyina.

Mala was pleasant company, and Sui Zi enjoyed chatting with her on a variety of topics as they traveled. Like the other children Sui Zi had accompanied on this trip, Mala was hungry. Although she never asked for food, she did not turn down any that was offered; then she ate very quickly. Sui Zi told Mala she would have plenty of food and love at the children's home. "Pastor Bawi and Seng Awn Lungjung take the children's education seriously, and you will be challenged to catch up to your age group in school and will be doing tuition classes to help."

After fifteen hours of travel, they finally came to the Mandalay station and exited the train. Pastor Bawi waved as the train came in and eagerly greeted Sui Zi and Mala. Seng Awn Lungjung and Pastor Bawi's wife accompanied him. Pastor Bawi greeted Mala and gave her a light hug, then they headed to the car for the ride to the children's home. As they drove, Pastor Bawi pointed out the school Mala would attend, and her eyes lit up upon seeing the large school building. He also pointed out the church and the area where the new children's home was being built.

Sui Zi exclaimed, "Oh, much work has already been done! I would love to walk over there and pray for the building."

"We will take a walk to the site before you have to leave us," Pastor Bawi assured her.

When they arrived at the apartments where Pastor Bawi lived with the children, the children came running to meet Mala. Other children whom Sui Zi had brought to live here circled her – some to say hello and others to inquire of news from home. Sui Zi laughed. "Slow down, slow down. I will be here for several days, and we can catch up during that time."

Seng Awn Lungjung introduced the children to Mala while one young lady, Bawk Sun, stood back from the group. She waited to meet Mala, show her around the home, and help her adjust to living there. She was the last to be introduced to Mala and greeted her with a big smile. Bawk Sun was fourteen years old and came from Chin State. "Come with me and I will show you to our room."

Seng Awn Lungjung stopped the two girls and gave Bawk Sun instructions. "Make sure you give Mala toiletries and any clothing she needs. Show her where to clean up, then come back down at dinnertime."

Mala and Bawk Sun were already getting along fine. Sui Zi loved how God guided Pastor Bawi's matching of children to be friends; she had never seen one combination not work. Sui Zi took advantage of this break and went to Seng Awn Lungjung's apartment to clean up and rest from the long trip.

A wonderful dinner of celery and mustard leaves with curry chicken and rice was served. As Sui Zi caught up on the news of the children's home, she watched to see how Mala was doing. Bawk Sun and Mala were giggling and talking of girl things. Bawk Sun had given Mala a Hello Kitty barrette. Mala was clean and in new clothes, and she wore her new barrette. Sui Zi overheard Mala ask about chores. Bawk Sun said, "We do not have many chores. Tuition classes are the hardest part of living here because they involve much studying. Pastor Bawi wants us to do well in school. He will take you in the morning to the local government offices to have pictures taken and identify you as living in the children's home."

The new children found this to be the hardest part of adjusting. They were scared to go to the military and get registered. Most of these children had seen or heard of the military violence.

Many had fathers who fought in the KIA, and they were taught that the military rule was wrong. So to go to the offices for identification was a scary time for them. Pastor Bawi always tried to explain the process and the reason they had to be registered. The military required Pastor Bawi to do certain things as an NGO. He had to agree to register each child, which included the military taking pictures of the child. There were also rules that he could not run a church out of the children's home. He was allowed to raise the children as Christians if they came to the home as Christians. The military always asked this question. Pastor Bawi followed all the government rules because if he did not, he risked losing his NGO status and ability to help the children. He stayed on friendly terms with the local military leaders he worked with in order to support his mission.

Sui Zi prayed while Pastor Bawi and Mala went to the military office. She knew this was a hard time for the child. Pastor Bawi always waited until their second full day at the home to take them for registration. It was better to have the child adjusted from the travel and looking rested and healthy for pictures. They soon returned, and Mala was off to her tuition class with Bawk Sun.

Seng Awn Lungjung told Sui Zi that Mala would have no trouble catching up to Standard 9 with the other girls her age. "She is very intelligent and is doing well in the Standard 9 tuition class. Mala will also attend an accelerated Standard 8 tuition class to prepare her for that testing. Mala will be very busy for the next few months, so she can start in Standard 9 when classes resume. I agree with you that Mala behaves older than her fourteen years. She came to me asking what chores she had to do to help. She was surprised that she only needed to take care of her laundry and the room. I told her there were no chores that she had to do. It is obvious that Mala is used to hard work." Sui Zi was pleased that Mala was adjusting so well.

That afternoon Pastor Bawi and Sui Zi walked to the building site of the new children's home. As they walked, Sui Zi filled Pastor Bawi in on Mala's story. He said, "It is sad to hear that the fighting has intensified in Kachin and Chin States. I came from Chin State and hope for peace and freedom for my people. I have now raised one hundred percent of the funds for building the new home." He was excited to show Sui Zi the plans and the good progress on the building. They walked around the site and prayed for God's blessing on the project and for the children who would live in this new home.

"Some of the girls are not excited about the new children's home, and they have asked to stay with my family. Please pray about how to handle this situation. I've always treated the children as a part of my family and do not want to force the children to go to the new home. In my personal apartment space, we could keep three or four girls, but I don't want to separate the children or cause issues."

"My husband and I will surely pray, and I know our church will pray about this issue also. I am sure God will direct you to the right solution," Sui Zi said.

The next day Sui Zi said goodbye to Mala and all of the other children. Pastor Bawi's driver waited to take her to the train station, as Sui Zi told Pastor Bawi he did not need to accompany her; she would be fine. He had much to do with overseeing the building and raising all of these children. He also taught tuition classes and preached in a home church in the city. Even so, Pastor Bawi accompanied Sui Zi to the train station. He stayed with her until the train came and stood on the platform where he waved goodbye as the train pulled away. Sui Zi thought Pastor Bawi was a wonderful man of God. She prayed for him and Hope Christian Children's Home until the rocking of the train eased her into a deep sleep.

Khuang Ja

The busy week made Sui Zi look forward to having a cup of tea and bread on her way home. She walked into the open area of Tial Hniang's tea shop and took a seat at a table. Tial Hniang was Pastor Bawi's cousin, and Sui Zi frequented the tea shop to help this family in their transition. They had managed an alcohol shop in Chin State, but Pastor Bawi worked hard with Tial Hniang and the local pastor to relocate them and turn them away from selling alcohol. The change made life hard for Tial Hniang and her family because she made more money selling alcohol than she did with the tea shop. Her husband was paralyzed and unable to work, so Tial Hniang supported herself, him, and their three children. One son, Khuang Ja, had been in Sui Zi's class at school, and she had grown close to him.

Khuang Ja was working with his mother at the tea shop that day, and he gave Sui Zi one of his great smiles that lit up his whole face. Sui Zi always called him Smiley Face. "How is your day going?" she asked him.

"It has been a very busy day. I attended school this morning after helping Mother get Father ready for the day. Taking care of Father is hard work. He cannot walk at all now, and our family must care for him in all ways. I am in charge of helping him with the bathroom and cleaning him up. Mother feeds him and does other things. Sometimes I see that Mother is very tired, and I tell her to eat while I feed Father. My younger sister and brother are not able to help because Father needs to be carried or pushed and dragged in his chair. I wish we could get him a chair with wheels. That would make moving him much easier."

"You must be very strong in order to move your father." Sui Zi was rewarded with another one of his great smiles.

Sui Zi did not know what was wrong with Khuang Ja's father, but she did not pry. People in this culture are not nosey; they wait for others to tell them. If they didn't say anything, Sui Zi thought she didn't need to know. She watched the emotions fly across Khuang Ja's face as he discussed caring for his father. This was not an easy situation for this child to handle or for his mother. Sui Zi thought Tial Hniang looked much older than her age because she had a hard life of caring for her husband and supporting her children. The school costs were only going to get higher as the children moved into secondary school, but she was glad that Tial Hniang was out of the alcohol business and running this tea shop.

Sui Zi wanted to ask Khuang Ja about a situation she had heard about in school – that he had been fighting with some of the Buddhist children. She was concerned that Khuang Ja was getting into physical fights with the boys. Boys from Chin State had the reputation of being excellent fighters and were prone to use their fists to solve problems. Since Khuang Ja's family relocated here from Chin State, she wanted to make sure that Khuang Ja knew that fistfights were not a good way to solve problems. When he returned to the table with Sui Zi's slice of bread and a small cup of strong tea, she asked him to join her for a few minutes.

"Khuang Ja, I heard you were in a fight with some of the Buddhist boys at school," she said to him outright.

"Four boys in my class were giving me a hard time about being a Christian. They made fun of me for believing in Jesus. They said Jesus was a horrible thief, and because of that, He was hung to die on a cross. They said I worshipped a thief."

"What did you do when those boys said that to you?" Sui Zi was concerned he would say he hit them.

Instead, Khuang Ja responded, "I said, 'So what, you worship a stupid golden statue! Nothing but a stupid statue made of gold.'" Sui Zi was relieved that he had not used his fists to put those boys in their place. Sui Zi said, "I am pleased that you have used words and did not have a physical fight with the boys." Khuang Ja smiled before going back to helping his mother.

As she drank her tea, Sui Zi decided to ask Tial Hniang if she would like to send Khuang Ja and his sister Numri Pan to Pastor Bawi's home for secondary school. She knew that Tial Hniang would not be able to continue their education, and with the expansion of the children's home, they might be able to go as Christian hardship cases. They had both been in her classroom in Class 3, and they were bright and hardworking students.

She thought Pastor Bawi would welcome the children as a way to ease the family's burden, since Tial Hniang was barely getting by on the money from the tea shop. She knew there were days that the family only had one meal, and if they had three meals, they were mostly rice with a few vegetables. Sui Zi often felt bad when she saw Khuang Ja or his sister hungrily watching her eat her bread with her tea. Sometimes she purchased bread for them and told them to take a break and join her. It was a little thing she could do to help them. She and Pastor Bawi did not want to see Tial Hniang go back to selling alcohol for a living. The Christian community frowned upon the selling of alcohol; the church family did not accept them either, if they did so. Everyone supported and helped them as much as possible after they switched to a tea shop.

After she finished her tea and bread, Sui Zi went over to Tial Hniang and discussed many things. They talked about the weather, the children, and their finances since Tial Hniang started the tea shop. Sui Zi noticed the age lines in Tial Hniang's face; she was aging quickly as she cared for an invalid husband and her children.

"Have you ever thought of sending Khuang Ja and Numri Pan to Pastor Bawi and the children's home?" Sui Zi asked.

"I have not thought about it. I thought all the children there were orphans."

Sui Zi explained, "Some of the children there are Christian hardship cases, and I think your children would qualify under these circumstances for secondary schooling."

Tial Hniang said, "There is no way I can send the children to secondary school; it is too costly."

"Would you be able to care for your husband and youngest child without the older two children to help?"

"It would be more difficult because Khuang Ja helps with his father. His paralysis has become worse over the last two years. It started with just some of his extremities, but now his entire body below the neck is not functioning without assistance.

"I know that Khuang Ja has already told you how his father

cannot feed, bathe, or care for himself. Everything has to be done for him. I took him to the doctor, but there is no help for him."

"Did you take him to the hospital for evaluation by their doctors?"

"No, I took him to the clinic. Their opinion is that his spine was injured, which causes the difficulties. There is no way we can afford the hospital."

"I think you should inquire at Myitkyina General Hospital to see if you can get help for your husband. You could also talk with the pastor; maybe someone in the church could assist. The hospital is probably costly, but the clinic is not a good place to go for a serious medical condition. Try the hospital, Tial Hniang; you are fortunate in your city to have a one.

"In the villages in Chin and Kachin States, there are no clinics or hospitals. Maybe his spine injury cannot be fixed, but there might be services that could help your family. Maybe you can get a wheelchair to help move him."

"Yes," Tial Hniang admitted, "I do have trouble carrying him from place to place, and a wheelchair would make it much easier."

"I will ask Pastor Bawi to see if he can get a used wheelchair in Mandalay," Sui Zi told her. "And I will speak with Pastor Bawi about everything you have told me."

Several weeks passed, and Sui Zi had her monthly conversation with Pastor Bawi to check on the progress of the children and discuss many issues that faced the Christian community in Kachin and Chin States. "I have been to Tial Hniang's tea shop several times over the past month and discussed the possibility of sending Khuang Ja and Numri Pan to the children's home for their secondary care and support," Sui Zi said.

Pastor Bawi responded positively. "This is a good idea; they should be able to relocate to the children's home after the school year ends at summer break. That way they can take tuition classes during the summer and prepare for the upcoming school year."

Then they discussed the possibility of helping Tial Hniang get funds for having her husband checked out at the hospital and purchasing a wheelchair. Pastor Bawi said, "I will work to find a wheelchair for him. If I am able, my wife and I will go visit them and discuss the possible relocation of the children with Tial Hniang. Thank you for looking out for my family."

Then they discussed the status of the building project and the progress of the children in their studies and health. Pastor Bawi said, "The children are all very busy with the school's tuition classes; the boys like to play futball while the girls prefer badminton. Many nights I hear the boys talking about their futball games and favorite teams. If I am successful in finding a used wheelchair, maybe we can come during the October Thadingyut holiday." Thadingyut is a Buddhist holiday. It lasts for three days, which would give them time to go to the village and get back before classes resumed.

Thadingyut came fast, and Sui Zi waited at the train station to greet Pastor Bawi and his family. Ja San had brought the cab to transport them back to their apartment where they would stay for two nights. When the train arrived, Sui Zi waved to Pastor Bawi as the train passed by and then stopped at the station. Since he had seen her, she patiently waited for them to disembark and make their way back to where she waited for them on the platform.

Sui Zi had not told Tial Hniang yet about the wheelchair that Pastor Bawi had purchased for her husband. She wanted it to be a surprise. Tial Hniang thought Pastor Bawi was coming to discuss the children and see how she was doing in her new establishment. As Pastor Bawi's family headed toward Sui Zi, she saw that they pushed a beautiful wheelchair with their luggage piled on top. This would change Khuang Ja and his family's routine – no more carrying or dragging their father around. This was a true answered prayer. Sui Zi thought about how she, her husband, and the entire church had prayed that God would provide this wheelchair for him.

After the greetings, they all piled into the cab and drove to Sui Zi's apartment. They were tired from the journey and thankful for the meal and tea that Sui Zi had planned for them. After they had eaten and rested, Sui Zi and Pastor Bawi headed to Tial Hniang's tea shop with the wheelchair. Tial Hniang spotted them as they walked up the path to her shop, nestled in the middle of the slum. Tial Hniang, who was not prone to displays of emotion, started to cry. She was so surprised, she asked, "How much did the wheelchair cost? I have very little money for such an item."

"It is a gift from the church and God," Pastor Bawi told her.

There was relief and thankfulness etched on her face. "Let's go show my husband." She called for Khuang Ja, and when he came from the back of the shop, she asked, "Will you watch the tea shop while we take the wheelchair to the back and show it to Father?"

Khuang Ja smiled as he gave Pastor Bawi a great big hug. "Thank you for your care for our family."

Soon Tial Hniang came back, wheeling her husband into the tea shop. "No more will he spend his days sitting in the chair or lying in the bed," she exclaimed. "This wheelchair will enable us to bring him into the tea shop." He still could not roll himself due to the loss of mobility of his arms, but he could come and converse with customers and be with his family. "Maybe we can even go out more with the ability to push him along," she added.

They all sat at a table, and Khuang Ja served them tea and toast. They got caught up on how everyone was doing. Pastor Bawi discussed current news stories and read a story from the day's paper that he brought from the capital. News was a very important part of Myanmar life, and since television was limited, the newspaper was vital and widely read even though the three main newspapers in Myanmar were owned and controlled by the military government. After reading the article, Pastor Bawi discussed the possibility of bringing the children to his home for their secondary education. Pastor Bawi wanted to know what Tial Hniang and her husband thought about the idea.

"With the new wheelchair, it would be easier for us to handle his care without Khuang Ja," she said.

Pastor Bawi added, "It is often easier for children who have siblings with them to transition to the home when they have someone familiar with them."

Tial Hniang said, "I talked with both children, and they have reservations about leaving. I think it would help if you could talk with them, Pastor."

"Also, the children can come home on breaks and spend the time with their family," he told them. "Unlike other children who have nowhere to go for the summer break and holidays, Khuang Ja and his sister would be an exception and could come home for some of the breaks, as long as they kept up with their studies."

Tial Hniang liked that idea and thought the children would too.

"I will come back in the morning and talk to Khuang Ja and Numri Pan about this," he said.

The next morning Pastor Bawi and Sui Zi walked back to the tea shop. Khuang Ja and Numri Pan were waiting to talk with them. Sui Zi noticed that they were not greeted with one of Khuang Ja's beautiful smiles. The children were quiet and nervous. Pastor Bawi greeted them and asked if the wheelchair had helped. Khuang Ja spoke up. "It makes it easier to get Father about. I used wood to make a ramp to roll the chair in and out of our shack at the back of the shop."

"Maybe you can be an engineer one day," Pastor Bawi said.

Khuang Ja insisted he was going to be a famous futball player. Then they went into a long discussion on futball and their favorite teams. "I am the best forward," Khuang Ja said, "and I'm always asked to play when a game gets going at school or at home."

Pastor Bawi told him that they could use a good forward at the children's home. That was a good lead-in to discuss what the home would be like and how it could help them. Pastor Bawi shared with the children about the new home that was being built. "If you come, you will be given a choice to live at my home with my family or at the children's home. At the home, you would share a room with other children – Khuang Ja with other boys and Numri Pan with other girls. There will be six children in a room. Everyone gets their own bed and place to store their clothes and belongings. You will have three meals a day and free tuition classes to help you pass your exams."

Khuang Ja started asking questions about tuition classes. "I know some of the kids at my school get tuition classes from the teachers to help them pass the tests. We have never had a tuition class."

Pastor Bawi told him, "Every day you will have tuition classes at the children's home in addition to your school classes. In tuition classes, you will stay ahead of the schoolwork you are doing in your class to make sure you are prepared and have memorized the subject carefully and correctly. Each subject you are required to learn for your class will be covered in detail during tuition classes. The children's home will pay for your clothes and nice school uniforms. You will get school supplies and an allowance. You can use the allowance to help the teacher at school if funds are needed for the teacher. Or, if your teacher does not need the funds that week, you can spend the money on things you would like. What are your favorite foods to eat?"

Khuang Ja quickly answered, "Fried eggs and bread or fried chicken."

Numri Pan said, "I like all food I am given to eat."

"You do not have to decide today, but think about how it could be good for you and your family. Your mother would not have to worry about where to get the money for your tuition, and it would free up funds for the family to have extra food for the three who are left back home working. Your younger sister could come to the home when she approaches secondary school age. We do all we can to help our children go to either the university or Bible college."

Once again Khuang Ja stated, "I want to be a famous futball player and do not need further education."

Pastor Bawi smiled at Khuang Ja and said, "Well, let's say that doesn't work out; what is your second choice?"

Khuang Ja said, "I'd like to be a pastor like the one from our church and you." This brought a huge smile to Pastor Bawi's face as he encouraged the boy to follow Jesus and serve in His church.

When asked, Numri Pan said, "I want to be a schoolteacher like Sui Zi."

Pastor Bawi assured both children that by coming to the children's home, he would work with them to make sure they became a pastor and a teacher. Then Khuang Ja asked, "What about being a famous futball player?"

Pastor Bawi said, "You will get to play a ton of futball with other children."

Tial Hniang came over and said it was time for the children to get their chores done. The children ran off to do their chores, and Tial Hniang asked Pastor Bawi how the discussion had gone. "I am certain," he began, "that the children will decide to come to the home."

Tial Hniang said, "I will miss them greatly, but there is no way I can afford their secondary school. It would help with the family's resources if I didn't have to feed the two children, especially Khuang Ja who seems to always be hungry and the first one done eating."

"The children will have three meals a day and snacks. Plenty of protein and fresh fruit."

"That is more than they get now. My husband said that he would miss the children, but it would be best for everyone and quite an opportunity for them to get an education. That could change our family's life."

"We are going to visit some friends in the area for the afternoon," Pastor Bawi told her, "but my wife and I will stop by in the morning before leaving on the train. If your family's decision is yes, you should plan for the children to come after the rainy season and before school starts next summer break."

The next morning before breakfast, Sui Zi, Ja San, and Pastor Bawi's family all prayed and thanked God for this trip and time together, and prayed for His wisdom and guidance in bringing Khuang Ja and Numri Pan to the children's home. They prayed that Tial Hniang would find proper medical care for her husband and for God's healing grace. They prayed for travel mercies for Pastor Bawi and his family as they headed back home.

After this prayer time, the entire group headed to Tial Hniang's tea shop to get the answer on whether or not Khuang Ja and Numri Pan would be coming to the children's home. When they arrived this time, they were greeted by one of Khuang Ja's beautiful smiles. Sui Zi exclaimed, "There is my Smiley Face!"

Khuang Ja went up to Pastor Bawi and said, "It has been decided that my sister and I will come to the children's home for secondary education." He seemed at peace with the decision and not nervous as he had been the day before.

"This is great news," Pastor Bawi told Khuang Ja and Numri Pan, "and I will be looking forward to the day that you come and join us next year."

As Pastor Bawi waited for the train to arrive, he said to Sui Zi, "I look forward to the day when you bring Khuang Ja and Numri Pan."

Sui Zi said, "The time will pass quickly as it seems to every year. I hope to hear that Khuang Ja chooses the university or Bible college over pursuing a career of a futball player."

Pastor Bawi smiled and said, "I am sure by the time we are done working with him, he will understand how few become famous futball players. I think Khuang Ja will be a great pastor someday."

Sui Zi agreed. "He has a heart for Jesus and cares for people, along with a beautiful smile that would all make good attributes for a pastor."

Lang Meng and Cin Vang

During the time that Sui Zi gave Burmese language classes at the refugee camp, she had become quite enamored with two of her young students, twelve-year-old Lang Meng and her thirteen-year-old friend Cin Vang. The two girls were inseparable in the camp. Sui Zi enjoyed having them in her class and found them to be quick learners. Both girls came from the same village in Kachin State and spoke a dialect that Sui Zi was familiar with, so they had several long conversations.

They had come to live in the refugee camp when the military army came into their village, and they had fled for their lives. As they left, they said they looked back and saw their village and all their belongings going up in flames. Everything was destroyed, so they came to the refugee camp with just the clothes on their backs. The girls had a long history together since they came from the same village; they each worked with their families in the rice patty fields and attended the same school but were one year apart in grades.

Cin Vang was the first child born from her mother's second marriage and one of seven children. Her mother had three children from her first marriage and four children from her second marriage. Cin Vang said, "Our family was very poor, and when the fighting got close to our village, my mother was concerned that her two eldest sons, who were ten and twelve years old, would be taken by the army and forced into the military. The military had taken many young boys and forced them to fight. The villagers were concerned about their boy children being forced into the military. They worried their daughters would be hurt in other horrific ways as the military ravaged their villages in search of rebel army members, so we hurried and left everything behind to escape the village."

Cin Vang's family was packed into one small room at the refugee camp. Sui Zi thought it was good that Cin Vang spent much time with Lang Meng since she and her grandparents had more room. As Sui Zi talked with Cin Vang's mother and stepfather about sending her to the children's home, the mother asked to send her oldest sons to the school also.

Sui Zi had to explain the situation. "Since the boys have not attended school since moving into the refugee camp and had little schooling before coming to the camp, they would not do well in the school. It would be hard for them. Cin Vang not only did well in the village school, she also worked to attend the classes at the refugee camp. Cin Vang is very intelligent and would do well in school."

The stepfather then said, "Since Cin Vang is my oldest child, I'd like her to have the opportunity. She'd be able to get work and help the family with this opportunity. I appreciate your kind words of praise for her and recognition of her intelligence."

"I would like to think about it and talk to Cin Vang before we make a decision," added Cin Vang's mother.

"I would be glad to come back and be a part of the discussion with Cin Vang if you would like," Sui Zi told her.

Cin Vang's friend Lang Meng was an only child who had been abandoned to live with her maternal grandparents when she was two years old. Her mother and father had divorced and left her.

"I don't remember my mother or father," she told Sui Zi. "I only know my grandparents. They told me that my mother and father divorced and moved to other villages. My life with my grandparents in the village is nice. They work in the rice patty fields. When I am not in school, I spend my days working alongside my *a phua*. My favorite times in the village are when I sing with *A Phua* while we work. My *a bo* is very kind to me; he talks with me about school and church.

"We fled the village as the government military approached, so we were not able to take anything with us – only the clothes we were wearing. I smelled the smoke from the burning village and saw the fire and smoke as we ran. I was afraid for myself and my grandparents but thankful that Jesus protected us. We escaped with the other villagers and made the long journey to the refugee camp."

Sui Zi then talked with Lang Meng's grandparents about her leaving the refugee camp and going to the children's home to attend school. They said, "We will pray because it is a big decision. We are getting older and worry about what would happen to Lang Meng if we were to pass away. We know she is very smart; we sent her to school so she might learn as much as she could.

"What is life like at the children's home? Will there be enough food when she is hungry? We only have two meals a day here, and she is always hungry."

"There will be three meals a day that would include vegetables and meat," Sui Zi told them. The *a bo* was glad to hear that the food would be better for her.

"She will also have clothes and school uniforms," Sui Zi continued. "The home will pay her tuition and school fees along with books and supplies. She will even have a weekly allowance that she can use to help at school or get little things for herself. She will attend church and a weekly Bible class at the children's home."

The *a phua* shared that Lang Meng loved to sing in church, and her favorite hymn was "You Are My All in All." Sui Zi saw relief slowly appear on their faces as they talked about the possibility for Lang Meng to have this opportunity. Sui Zi left them with a promise to come back to hear their decision.

A week passed and Sui Zi went back to the refugee camp. She was greeted quickly by Lang Meng and Cin Vang who had questions about the children's home. Sui Zi was pleased and surprised that both girls knew they would be going to live at the children's home. Neither one looked scared, and both seemed excited to talk to her.

After class, Sui Zi and the girls sat down to discuss everything from the trip to the home and all aspects of life at the children's home. The only hint of sadness was when Lang Meng realized she would not be able to visit or see her grandparents. She was quite attached to them and helped care for them. Sui Zi told her, "Your grandparents will be watched out for by the other Christians in the camp. I will bring news of them to you whenever I come to visit the children's home."

This seemed to ease Lang Meng's concerns for her grandparents. Sui Zi then went with the girls to make sure their parents and grandparents all agreed. After a complete agreement was verified, Sui Zi left the refugee camp to call Pastor Bawi to see when they could make their move to the children's home.

They decided that Sui Zi could bring the girls on the next break from school that was coming in two weeks. She would take the girls on the usual route via the train. The girls were excited when Sui Zi went to the refugee camp and told them the news. Lang Meng's grandparents seemed sad to hear it would happen so quickly. Cin Vang's family seemed pleased to hear that she would be going soon to start her education in the city. Sui Zi reminded them, "You do not have to worry about funds; the children's home will cover all the travel costs and provide the things the girls need for school and tuition classes. The home will even provide clothes and supplies."

In two weeks Sui Zi was at the train station with these two excited young ladies. The girls chatted away about the journey. There were no tears shed, and both girls were interested in travel and the train ride. Neither had ridden on a train before and this was a big event. They watched all the people as they waited at the train station. Sui Zi made sure they had plenty to eat and drink. Soon they boarded the train and were off on their journey.

Sui Zi had tins of rice, vegetables, and chicken for them to eat on the trip. She also had money for extra food and snacks. Cin Vang and Lang Meng were on an adventure together, away from the crowded refugee camp, and they were excited to be going. Sui Zi thought about how some children cried and others were quiet, but not Lang Meng and Cin Vang. They chatted away in their excitement. Sui Zi was glad to be going to the children's home to see everyone and excited to see the progress in the new home. Pastor Bawi had told her it was almost complete.

With the fifteen-hour journey behind them, they arrived at the train station to the warm greeting of Pastor Bawi and his wife. The girls immediately took to the pastor's wife. She talked with them about new clothes and barrettes. Pastor Bawi asked them how they enjoyed the trip, and the girls were quick to describe all the details of the trip. Sui Zi realized it was good that the two friends came together.

Once they were back at the apartments where Pastor Bawi, his family, and all the children lived in a series of rented apartments, Sui Zi inquired about the children's home. Pastor Bawi said, "First we have dinner and rest. In the morning I will take you to see our progress."

Over dinner they discussed the children and how studies were going. They also talked about a small country children's home that churches supported. "They have an opening for a young boy," Pastor Bawi said. "If you know of anyone who would be a good fit, please let me know. How are Tial Hniang and the rest of the family doing?"

"They are all well, and the plans are in place to bring Khuang Ja and Numri Pan when this school session ends."

"That is wonderful. They will be among the first children to live in the new home."

Early the next morning Pastor Bawi and Sui Zi walked through the slum to the edge of the site where the children's home was being built. The building was almost complete, and painting was going on in the lower half of the building. The size of the building amazed Sui Zi, and they discussed how he would manage to care for so many additional children.

"I have plans to hire a director, cook, and staff to help care for the children. They will live at the children's home." He showed Sui Zi their quarters and the layout for the boys' section of the home and the girls' section of the home. He continued, "There will be large rooms with blackboards across the walls for tuition classes, and a kitchen and dining hall with a TV too." It was a beautiful new children's home, and Sui Zi was pleased to see God blessing the work of Pastor Bawi and his wife with the children.

Sui Zi spent time with the children she had brought to the home and answered all the questions she could about news from home. She had updates for some but not for others. She could tell them of the happenings in their areas, however. Lang Meng and Cin Vang appeared to be adjusting to the new home. They showed Sui Zi their new clothes and barrettes. They were each given toiletries and mats to sleep on and were excited that they would have beds in the new children's home. Both girls were quite taken with Pastor Bawi's infant son. Pastor Bawi's wife joked that she would never get a chance to hold him with these two girls around. They seemed to be enjoying meeting the other children as well.

The next day Sui Zi headed to the train station to make the long trip home. She thought she would miss Lang Meng and Cin Vang. They had been great travel companions on the way down, and she had enjoyed having them in Burmese classes at the refugee camp. She praised God for giving Lang Meng and Cin Vang the opportunity to come to this home and get an excellent education but, more importantly, to grow in their knowledge of Jesus and following Him.

Dua Lian Hmung

Two weeks after Sui Zi returned home, her good friend Pastor Laseng Raw called her. She always enjoyed talking with him, for he had a wonderful sense of humor. He also had a compassionate heart toward the children; he laughed at their playfulness and prayed for the sick ones. Though he and his small church cared for and supported the children's home, he apologized that they had so little to give the home.

When he called, however, he had a request. "There is an orphan boy in Chin State who needs a home. He has no relatives to care for him, and a pastor reached out to us and asked if there was room in one of the children's homes for him."

Sui Zi responded quickly. "A room is available for a new boy at Grace Christian Children's Home."

"That is wonderful. I will have the pastor from Chin State call you to discuss the boy further." In the meantime, Sui Zi called Kaw Jar at Grace Christian Children's Home to verify that there was still room for another boy at their home. Kaw Jar had more to share with Sui Zi. "It would be nice to visit with you. The children's home has been having some hard times, but by God's grace we are making it through the tough times. The man from the United States who had provided the funds for the building of this home on my land is terminally ill with cancer and will no longer be able to help with monthly support. The Christian churches across Myanmar that I work with are all sending what they can to help. We will talk more when you come. Please pray for God to keep providing for the children's needs." Sui Zi would of course be praying.

As soon as the call ended, Sui Zi and her husband bowed their heads and joined hands in prayer. Sui Zi prayed, "Father God, we lift up the American sponsor of Grace Christian Children's home and ask for you to heal him of his cancer. We ask you to bless him for all he has been able to do for the children at the home. Father, please give Kaw Jar peace as she faces the many financial challenges of running the home and caring for the children at the home and in the university. Father, many churches in Myanmar do their best to help; please bless them with the ability to assist more during this time. We trust you Lord to work on behalf of Grace Christian Children's home and bring what they need to continue raising children that follow you. We pray a blessing for the children being supported at the home and ask that you continue to watch out for them, especially the children now attending University. We also pray for the children we have yet to meet that you will be calling us to work with in the future. Father, we thank you for all you have done and will continue to do for the children of Myanmar. Father God, we ask these things in the precious name of your Son Jesus Christ, and it's in His name we pray, Amen."

The next morning the pastor from Chin State called to talk with Sui Zi about one of the children in his village, Dua Lian Hmung. "He is a twelve-year-old boy whose parents have died. His mother died during a miscarriage when he was two years old, and his father died last month from malaria. Neither parent had any living family. I took Dua Lian Hmung in to live with my family until a place in a children's home could be found. He is a very talented boy and loves to sing in church. His prized possession is an old guitar his father had given him. The boy practices until he figures out a song on the guitar; he has quite a good ear. He has taught himself how to play the guitar, is quick to smile, and loves to play futball."

Sui Zi explained more to the pastor. "Grace Christian Children's Home is in a rural area. The home was built by an American on Kaw Jar's property. Kaw Jar is a widow and manages the children's home along with a director and a cook.

"Kaw Jar lives in her original home on the property, which includes a main building where tuition classes are held but which also serves as the dining/kitchen area. There are also two dorm buildings, one for boys and the other for girls. Both have attached showers and toilet facilities. Currently this well-established home has nine boys and fourteen girls and has already sponsored two children through the university and one through Bible college.

"They have a large garden where the children work to grow more vegetables and fruit for them to eat, and they make bead purses to sell at market for additional funds. The home is having some difficulty due to the American support ending, but the Christian churches affiliated with the home in Myanmar are working to keep the home going."

The pastor told Sui Zi more about Dua Lian Hmung. "That home sounds like a good fit for a boy like Dua Lian Hmung. He comes from a farming village, so he'd fit right in to the rural setting of Grace Christian Children's Home."

Sui Zi and the pastor agreed that he would bring Dua Lian Hmung in two weeks by bus from Chin State to Mandalay where she would meet them. Then they would go by car the rest of the way to Grace Christian Children's Home and stay a couple days while Dua Lian Hmung got settled in.

"It is amazing how when a child needs a home, the timing seems to coincide with a time when I can be away from my position as a teacher," Sui Zi said. "All the government holidays provide me with time to do God's work. I rarely have to use my time off. I know many teachers just do not show up, but I take my job seriously and want to be a good educator. Though I am not allowed to share Jesus in school, I manage to find a way. God is good and I trust Him to provide a way for me to help the children with the funds needed for the travel."

Two weeks later Sui Zi was back on the train and headed to Mandalay. This time she would not see Pastor Bawi and Hope Christian Children's Home. She had to hurry to the taxi that the pastor had arranged to pick her up and get to the bus station to wait for Dua Lian Hmung and his pastor's arrival. Sui Zi closed her eyes and prayed for the support needed for Grace Christian Children's Home and for Dua Lian Hmung's travel and adjustment to the changes he was facing.

After waiting for an hour, the bus arrived. Off came the pastor and a young boy carrying a guitar. Sui Zi knew this was Dua Lian Hmung and walked over to greet them. Dua Lian Hmung greeted her with a shy, beautiful, crooked-tooth smile. They decided to get some food before starting the two-and-a-half-hour drive to the home. The driver took them to a good area to find food, and they had soup with vegetables, bread, and tea. As they drove to Grace Christian Children's Home, Dua Lian Hmung fell asleep in the car, worn out from the travel and his belly full of good food.

The pastor said, "Dua Lian Hmung has never traveled outside his village. This trip by motorbike to the bus and now a car ride has been quite an experience for him. I'm just glad he did not experience motion sickness as some children do when they travel the first time."

They turned onto the rough, bumpy, dirt road that led to the children's home. When they stopped, twenty-three children came running from the garden, yard, and dorms to meet their new brother. Kaw Jar was happy to see her old friend Sui Zi and meet Dua Lian Hmung. Dua Lian Hmung held tightly to his guitar as he walked up to meet Kaw Jar. She introduced him to the other children and told him it would take time, but he would learn everyone's name.

As Kaw Jar took him to see his room, Sui Zi noticed that there were issues with the buildings. The porch wood had rotted through in several places. The wood floor in the dorms was worn through and rotting. Kaw Jar had placed heavy rugs over the holes, but it was evident the floors needed to be replaced. Dua Lian Hmung looked all around and seemed a little lost.

Kaw Jar asked, "Would you like to put the guitar down and play futball?"

Dua Lian Hmung set his things down where Kaw Jar showed him, and soon the boys were outside picking teams and positions. With Dua Lian Hmung they had ten boys to make up the two teams. The trees at each end of the yard served as the ends of the field, and the dorms on either side were the sidelines. They marked the goal lines in the dirt with sticks from the trees. The boys let Dua Lian Hmung play his favorite position as a forward. With each team having a goalie, two forwards, and two guards, the game began with their worn-out futball that barely held air. The boys played hard, as the girls watched; some of the girls played with dolls or braided each other's hair, and some made beaded purses.

Kaw Jar turned to the pastor and Sui Zi, "Would you like to join me for tea?"

As they settled in to have their tea, she explained the situation. "The American who funded the building of the dorms is dying of cancer. He will not be able to support the home any longer, and I am concerned about the rotting floors. I wish they had built the dorms of concrete instead of wood. The plan was to upgrade them over time to concrete buildings, but now we have lost our American funding. The wet weather in this part of Myanmar has caused the wood to rot quickly. Without the American's help, we have no way to make the repairs. Thankfully, the churches are providing some money to help keep the children in school, feed them, and meet their medical needs. We are also making bead purses to sell at the market to raise money. Things are tight, and I must make food stretch. Everyone is praying for a new international sponsor to come forward to help the home."

Sui Zi and Kaw Jar discussed that possibly Pastor Bawi would know someone who could help from the international community.

Soon it was dinnertime, and Sui Zi only ate a small amount, knowing this was a strain on the home's food resources. After dinner, Kaw Jar asked Dua Lian Hmung if he would lead them in worship. He brightened up and ran to get his guitar. He played wonderfully, and they all sang along with him as he led them in "You Are My All in All."

He told Kaw Jar, "This is my favorite song. We sang it in

our church, and I taught myself to play it by practicing until I got it right. I want to grow up and lead worship in the church."

"Well, I believe you just became the children's home worship leader. I would like it very much if you could lead us in worship every day."

The weekend went quickly. Dua Lian Hmung fit right into the children's home, and he quickly made friends and was glad to join in and help with the chores. The tuition teacher realized he was a couple years behind in grade, so they decided to start him in the fourth grade. They found him some new clothes from their storage, a school uniform, and school supplies. He was all set up and seemed right at home.

After a few weeks, Dua Lian Hmung had attended the local church. He especially enjoyed going there because they had a keyboard and another couple who led them in worship songs. Dua Lian Hmung paid close attention to learn all he could from them. The pastor told Sui Zi he was glad they were able to bring Dua Lian Hmung to the home and give him hope and a future. Kaw Jar asked Sui Zi and the pastor to pray for the children's home and that sponsorship would be found soon. She knew she would not be able to meet all the needs for much longer and make all the repairs. She was concerned about the children they were supporting in the university and Bible college too. The funds were running low.

Seng Nu

We must move quickly kept running through Sui Zi's mind as she packed a bag to leave for Chin State. She would be gone for the whole school break. Ja San was concerned for her safety, but Sui Zi reassured him. "God is with me and will protect us during this difficult trip. We must trust and pray. Pastor and I must rescue a twelve-year-old girl who is in a very dangerous situation. A pastor in a very remote village has made contact with us to help this little one. Her name is Seng Nu, an orphan who had been sent to live with her stepfather's brother's family where she has been repeatedly raped by her step-uncle.

Her *a phua* had sent her to live with the step-uncle three years ago. During that time, the *a phua* became concerned when Seng Nu became more and more distant and withdrawn. The *a phua* was raising Seng Nu's younger sister, Htoi Seng, who is four years old and had thought it would be best for Seng Nu to live with the step-uncle and help on their farm. The step-uncle had said that Seng Nu would be a huge help to his wife by cooking and caring for their children and working with them on their farm. He promised her *a phua* that she would go to school and have food to eat."

Sui Zi continued to explain more to Ja San the reason for the hurry. "Last time the *a phua* saw Seng Nu, she was not the same child as she had been, so she insisted that Seng Nu be allowed to spend her school break with her and Htoi Seng. When Seng Nu arrived, she was very quiet and hardly talked to her *a phua* and sister. After a couple of days Seng Nu opened up to her *a phua* and begged her not to send her back to live with her step-uncle. When the *a phua* finally got Seng Nu to tell her what was happening, her heart was broken and sick at what had happened to this beautiful girl. Not knowing what to do, she contacted her church pastor and asked for guidance.

"Her pastor suggested that she keep the step-uncle from taking the child by force. The best option was to try to place the child in a Christian children's home far away from Chin State. They know time is of the essence because the step-uncle will return for her at the end of the break. The village pastor contacted our pastor and now me.

"I know Pastor Bawi's family at Hope Christian Children's Home is the best place for her. He has experience from helping another girl who had been sexually abused; he will know how to help this young girl. I called Pastor Bawi and explained the little bit I know about Seng Nu's situation. Pastor Bawi agreed to take Seng Nu; he will be ready for us when we arrive."

Sui Zi and her pastor planned to stay one day and night in the village with Seng Nu and her *a phua* to give Seng Nu a chance to become familiar with Sui Zi. Then, when they arrived at the children's home, Sui Zi would stay until she had to return to teach at the end of the break. With this plan, she would be with Seng Nu for at least seven days.

They set off on a bus for Chin State and had a car waiting to take them to the village. As they traveled, Sui Zi and the pastor prayed for God's protection for Seng Nu and that the step-uncle would not return early to retrieve her. The *a phua*'s pastor had told them that sometimes the step-uncle came early to take Seng Nu back when she was visiting with her *a phua*. He would say she was needed back on their farm.

The travel went well and Sui Zi thanked God for travel mercies. Soon they entered a village surrounded by rice patties. The pastor met them and took them to meet Seng Nu's *a phua*. The house was a simple bamboo-and-wood shack with a tin roof like all the homes in the village. They entered the one-room shack where the *a phua* waited for them with her pastor's wife.

The *a phua* looked heartbroken, and Sui Zi's heart broke for this older woman. Sui Zi sat down on a mat near the *a phua* so they could talk, and the pastor's wife offered them tea. After she poured the tea, the pastor's wife left them alone to talk.

"I am so sorry," Sui Zi began, "that we are meeting under these hard conditions. Would you please tell me about Seng Nu?"

The *a phua* was silent for a while and took a sip of tea. She finally looked up at Sui Zi with tears in her eyes. "I am devastated that I missed what was happening to my beautiful granddaughter. I thought the step-uncle just cared for Seng Nu's wellbeing and was overly protective of her. I don't understand how he could have done this to a child, but I saw Seng Nu start to change. I thought maybe the step-uncle and aunt were making her work too hard or beating her. I never imagined something this horrible was happening."

"Can you tell me about Seng Nu's parents? What happened to them?" Sui Zi asked.

"I am Seng Nu's mother's mother. Her father was an addict and died when she was five years old from an opium drug overdose. At that time Seng Nu had a brother, Tlumang, who was twelve. Her mother remarried when she was six, and Htoi Seng was born when Seng Nu was eight years old. During that year, both her mother and stepfather died from malaria. I did my best to care for the children and keep Seng Nu in school. Tlumang went to China to get work, and he sent me money to help with the girls, but it was still not enough. When Seng Nu's step-uncle, her stepfather's younger brother, came for a second visit to check on us, he asked if Seng Nu could go live with them. They had three children, and Seng Nu was to help his wife with the children and the farm work.

"He promised me that she would still go to school and have plenty to eat. Since his village was only an hour away, we would be able to visit, and I thought this was a better situation for Seng Nu. I thought I could better care for Htoi Seng. I am too old to work in the rice patty fields, and the money that Tlumang sent was not enough. Not only would I have had one less mouth to feed, but I also wanted to make sure that Seng Nu stayed in school. We decided that Seng Nu should go with her step-uncle."

The *a phua* was shaking as she told her story. Sui Zi reached out, and they held each other's hands so she could continue the story. "The visits became less frequent over the three years that Seng Nu lived there, and each time she came home, she was more and more distant. She did not smile and seemed afraid to talk with me."

With tears flowing, *A Phua* went on. "I demanded that

Seng Nu come home and spend time with me and Htoi Seng. I thought she was depressed or overworked. I never imagined something this awful could happen. Seng Nu had always been a very outgoing child with a beautiful smile, and to see her now is heartbreaking.

"When she first got home, she was withdrawn and did not talk or want to play with Htoi Seng. At night she had nightmares and did not sleep well. She had a few accidents and urinated in her sleep. I was concerned, so I asked her what was wrong, but she wouldn't answer me.

"After a week of this, I knew from raising my own daughter that this was not normal behavior, and something was upsetting the child. I kept asking direct questions about life with her step-uncle and aunt, but she evaded answering when we talked. She said they did not make her work too hard, and yes, she was going to school, but she would not say why she was unhappy living there. When I kept asking her, she finally cried and asked me to please not make her go back to live there with them.

"I was very confused and thought maybe they were beating the child, so I asked her if they beat her. Seng Nu shook her head and kept crying. I asked if the aunt was mean to her, and again she shook her head and kept crying. Then I asked if the uncle was mean to her, and she cried harder. I told her it was okay for her to tell me what was happening with her step-uncle. I thought maybe he was mean to her; I was not prepared for what she finally told me. Seng Nu cried to me, 'He hurts me, he hurts me. He tells me if I tell anyone that he will hurt you and Htoi Seng.'"

"I was still not understanding and asked Seng Nu how he hurt her."

Seng Nu said, "At first he just touched me." She told her *a phua* where and how, and then *A Phua* realized he had raped her.

The *a phua* had tears running down her cheeks when she

told Sui Zi that she asked how often this happened. "Poor Seng Nu said he had been hurting her ever since he took her to live with him. He did this several times a week.

"After Seng Nu told me this, she curled herself up against me and cried until she finally fell asleep. I just sat there next to Seng Nu with my hand on her back and cried for her. I wanted to make this go away for her.

"I did not know what to do, so I asked my pastor for help. We discussed several options but decided it was best to get Seng Nu safely away from the step-uncle. He suggested that we look for a Christian children's home that could take her and help her complete her schooling. As an orphan, there would be several good options. I was concerned about Seng Nu's safety at the children's home."

Sui Zi told her about Pastor Bawi and his work with children. "He has another girl who had been sexually abused, and they have helped her. This girl has now finished school and is a teacher. She is doing very well."

"What about Htoi Seng?" the *a phua* asked. "What if he tries to take her when she is older? Could Htoi Seng go live with Seng Nu too?"

Sui Zi said, "Yes. Once Htoi Seng is six years old, she can go live at the children's home since she is a Christian orphan. Then Seng Nu and her sister could be together." This pleased the *a phua*, as she was aging and did not want to risk Htoi Seng falling into the hands of the step-uncle.

"I wish Tlumang was here to help deal with the step-uncle. The pastor in my village said he and other men from the church will make sure the step-uncle leaves when he comes for Seng Nu. They will handle him and send him back to his village. They will make it clear he is not to come back and that Seng

Nu has been sent away to school. He assured me that the stepuncle would be dealt with and doubted he would come back for Htoi Seng."

Sui Zi said, "When Htoi Seng is school age, I will make sure she can join Seng Nu at Hope Christian Children's Home."

Then the *a phua* asked, "Are you ready to meet Seng Nu? She is with her sister, and they are ready to come in and eat."

Sui Zi said, "Yes, I would love to meet her." In came two beautiful girls, one full of life and the other looking scared. Her eyes looked empty, and she hung her head; she would not make eye contact when *A Phua* introduced her to Sui Zi.

"Seng Nu, would you please sit with me for the evening meal?" Sui Zi asked.

Seng Nu sat with Sui Zi, but she did not seem to want to talk and she ate very little. Her *a phua* had already explained to her that she would be going to live with other orphans in a Christian children's home. Sui Zi tried to tell her about their upcoming trip and life in the children's home, even though she knew that Seng Nu would probably live with Pastor Bawi and his wife as did the other girl they rescued. Helping the severely abused children was a full-time job. Several children had lived with their family instead of the home to be given more help. Some moved straight into the children's home, others lived with Pastor Bawi's family for a while and then moved to the children's home, and some stayed with Pastor Bawi and became part of his family. It just depended on what the child needed.

Finally, it was time to sleep, and Sui Zi asked, "May I spend the night here with you? It might give Seng Nu more time to get to know me."

The *a phua* and Sui Zi got everyone settled on mats for the night. Sui Zi prayed for Seng Nu to sleep and not have nightmares that night. It was a long time before sleep came to Sui Zi because her heart was broken for Seng Nu and what had happened to this precious, orphaned girl. Her heart was also broken for the *a phua* to lose her only child, her daughter, to malaria, and to lose her grandson at an early age when he insisted on going to China to work, and being left with two little girls but unable to work in the rice patties any longer. She could not imagine the heartbreak this woman was enduring.

"I will see that the pastor gives you updates on how Seng Nu is doing. I assure you that Seng Nu will be well cared for, and when the time comes, Htoi Seng can join her. The girls will be reunited, given an education, and most importantly, raised as Christians."

Morning came quickly, and Sui Zi thanked the Lord that Seng Nu had slept well. They had a quick breakfast of rice and tea. Once again Sui Zi told Seng Nu about the trip. "We will travel by car, bus, and then train to Mandalay. We will see many sights on the way, and you will meet Pastor Bawi and his wife when we arrive. They have a baby boy named Siang Za Nawl." Sui Zi hoped to reassure her about where they were going.

The parting was difficult; Seng Nu clung to her *a phua*. Finally, her *a phua* pushed her back and told her to be strong. "I trust the pastor and Sui Zi that you will be safe at Hope Christian Children's Home. Jesus will be with you and watch over you. Remember, Htoi Seng will join you in a few years."

The *a phua* then gave Seng Nu a last kiss and put her in the car. Seng Nu settled against the door and would not look up. Sui Zi waved goodbye to the *a phua*. The journey was a long one, and during the trip Seng Nu spoke very little, ate very little, and drank very little. She did not look out the car, bus, or train windows; she kept her head down for the entire trip. Sui Zi tried to engage her in conversation and kept talking about her life and the children at Hope Christian Children's Home. Sui Zi hoped this would prepare Seng Nu for her new life.

Three days later they reached Mandalay, stepped off the

train, and true to his word, Pastor Bawi and his wife were at the station to meet them. Seng Nu now clung to Sui Zi. She seemed scared to meet Pastor Bawi and his wife. Sui Zi did not pull her away but said, "Seng Nu, I would like to introduce you to Pastor Bawi and his wife."

Pastor Bawi said, "Welcome, Seng Nu. It is nice to meet you."

Pastor's wife got down at eye level with Seng Nu. "I am so glad to meet you and have you come join our family. Are you thirsty or hungry?"

Seng Nu shook her head. "Well, perhaps later," the pastor's wife said. "Let's head back to our apartment. It will soon be Siang Za Nawl's feeding time."

Another car and a quick ride took them to Pastor Bawi's house. In the car Seng Nu stayed right by Sui Zi and was quiet the entire time. Pastor Bawi told her about different sights as they traveled. He pointed out the shops, school, and new children's home, and finally they arrived at his apartment. Unlike the other children Sui Zi brought, Seng Nu was not taken to Hope to meet other children. She was taken straight to the pastor's family home. His wife's mother was there to greet them with a wonderful meal. Pastor's wife introduced Seng Nu to her mother and baby Siang Za Nawl. Seng Nu looked but did not say anything.

"Would you like something to eat or drink?" the pastor's wife asked. Seng Nu again shook her head. Then Pastor's wife showed Seng Nu a mat where she could sit and rest while the rest of them ate. Halfway through the meal, the pastor's wife again offered Seng Nu food and water. Once again Seng Nu shook her head.

"Just let her be for now," Pastor Bawi told his wife. "Don't worry; she will eventually eat."

When the meal was done, the family went about things as usual, and Seng Nu stayed on her mat but seemed to be attentive to all that was going on. Another girl, Zung Par Lang, was also living with the pastor and his family instead of living in the children's home. She was home from tuition class and talked with the family. Pastor Bawi introduced them. "Seng Nu, this is Zung Par Lang; she lives in our home also. I hope you will become great friends."

Sui Zi noticed Seng Nu seemed to relax as she watched Zung Par Lang interact with the family. When she was asked to go with the pastor's wife to get ready for bed, she did as she was told. Then she came back carrying her own mat and with her hair combed and ready to sleep. Sui Zi and Seng Nu slept with their mats side by side.

The next day Seng Nu again got up and listened to the pastor's wife as she told her to go with Zung Par Lang and get ready for the day. She came back in her same clothes and sat in the same place as the day before. The day passed quickly, and Sui Zi became concerned because Seng Nu had not eaten or drunk since arriving. Pastor Bawi and his wife assured her that this sometimes happens with traumatized children. Sui Zi was still worried and prayed.

That night at dinner, the *a phua* took a plate of food and a cup of tea and put them next to Seng Nu. She told her to please eat some. Zung Par Lang sat down and started chatting away as she ate. Finally, Seng Nu ate some of the food and drank the cup of tea. She still was not talking, but Sui Zi had hope when she saw her eat and was thankful she still had two days left to stay.

The next day they bought clothes for Seng Nu. Pastor Bawi's wife took Seng Nu and gave her soap and the new clothes. "Please clean yourself with these and put on the new clothes. Let me know if you have any trouble."

Sui Zi thought Seng Nu might not do what she was told, but she finally came out – all cleaned up with the new clothes on.

Pastor Bawi's wife then asked, "May I put a Hello Kitty barrette in your hair?"

Seng Nu mumbled her first word since coming. "Yes."

That evening Seng Nu watched the baby, Siang Za Nawl, and smiled at his gurgling. Pastor Bawi's wife asked her if she would like to hold him. Seng Nu nodded. She carefully held him until he fell asleep. Then the *a phua* came, took him, and laid him down. When Zung Par Lang got home for dinner, she once again sat and talked with Seng Nu and the family about her day. Seng Nu ate all her food and drank her tea.

That night Seng Nu woke everyone in the middle of the night, screaming. Sui Zi was at her side and kept saying, "It's okay, Seng Nu; you're safe."

Pastor Bawi and his wife both knelt down and softly talked to her, reassuring her that she was safe, and nothing bad would happen to her in their home. Seng Nu finally reached out for Pastor Bawi's wife and clung to her and cried. Pastor Bawi looked over to Sui Zi and gave her a reassuring look, as if to say, "See? She is going to be okay."

That night Seng Nu moved her mat to sleep next to Pastor Bawi's wife and fell back into a quiet sleep with no more nightmares. She got up in the morning and ate breakfast. She was most interested in Siang Za Nawl, and when asked if she wanted to help with him, she nodded. She fed him his next bottle and seemed quite pleased to do it. Sui Zi wished she could stay longer, but it was time for her to go home, back to her husband and teaching jobs. Sui Zi told Seng Nu that she would be leaving but she'd be back to check on her soon. Seng Nu looked up from feeding Siang Za Nawl. She did not say anything, but Sui Zi was pleased that she had looked at her.

Pastor Bawi took Sui Zi to the train station. On the way, he said, "The last girl who had been sexually abused did not eat for three days after coming to us. I am pleased that Seng

Nu shows attachment to my wife and Siang Za Nawl. I believe these are very good signs. Don't worry about her; I will keep you updated on her progress."

Sui Zi was soon back on the train and heading home. This trip had left her emotionally exhausted but thankful that Seng Nu was now safe, and through Jesus she'd have hope and a future.

Sung Tha Chin

Pastor Bawi told Sui Zi that they now had room for more children because the new children's home was up and running. "Please let us know if any orphans who need placement come to the refugee camps." He had heard of several children who had been misplaced due to the landslides that destroyed areas and farms in Chin State.

Sui Zi responded, "Refugees are coming from the devastation in Chin State and from the ongoing warfare in Kachin State. I will absolutely let you know of any children who are orphans and need help."

Pastor Bawi also informed her of the progress Seng Nu was making. "She continues to improve and will start school this week. Her nightmares are not as frequent, and she now engages with the family."

Sui Zi told Pastor Bawi she would continue to pray daily for Seng Nu and was thankful to hear of her progress. That week when Sui Zi worked at the refugee camp, she asked the workers, "Are there any orphans who need assistance? There are openings at the children's home."

One of the workers spoke up. "I know of one little girl who came with her grandparents, father, stepmother, younger brother, and sister. Her name is Sung Tha Chin, and she is nine years old. I overheard the stepmother say to the father, 'Why should I care for her? I am not her mother.' The father and stepmother continue to argue about Sung Tha Chin, which divides them and puts a strain on the family."

Sui Zi thought it was a shame when people did not accept the children from a previous marriage, but this was common in Myanmar. Often children from previous marriages were sent away to live with grandparents or sent to schools away from the new family.

Sui Zi told the workers, "I'd like to meet Sung Tha Chin." They directed her to the area of the camp where she lived with her family. One of the workers volunteered to go along and introduce them. They crossed the crowded camp and entered a hallway with a row of rooms that all looked alike. They went to the room where the seven members of this family lived. The worker introduced Sui Zi as a teacher who volunteered in the camp. They asked if she could meet Sung Tha Chin.

The father introduced his family to them, and Sung Tha Chin was the oldest of the children. Sui Zi noticed that Sung Tha Chin did not make eye contact with her when introduced; she seemed to look right through her like she was bored or out of sorts. "May I spend some time with Sung Tha Chin and see where she is in her studies?" Sui Zi asked.

"Of course. Sung Tha Chin is very intelligent, and if something interests her, she learns everything she can about it."

Sui Zi asked what interested her, and quickly Sung Tha Chin answered in English. Sui Zi then asked, "How are you?"

In English, Sung Tha Chin answered, "Fine, thank you."

"Where did you learn English?" Sui Zi inquired.

Sung Tha Chin said, "I took a book from the school in our village, listened in on the class, and taught myself."

Sui Zi was impressed and asked, "Would you like to come with me and work on studies with me?"

Sung Tha Chin said yes, so Sui Zi told the father that Sung Tha Chin would be back in an hour, and he said that would be fine. Sung Tha Chin was a short, thin, nine-year-old girl. She wore her hair short like a boy and had a nice smile.

"Will you teach me English?" she asked Sui Zi, so they went over the words that Sung Tha Chin knew. Sui Zi was surprised at how much she had taught herself even if her pronunciation was a bit off. Sung Tha Chin also spoke Burmese and her native language. She had a gift for learning different languages. Sung Tha Chin told Sui Zi that languages interested her, so she learned them.

Sui Zi learned that Sung Tha Chin also liked school and enjoyed Sunday school. Sung Tha Chin said, "I like school as long as they keep teaching me."

"What do you mean?"

Sung Tha Chin said, "Memorization is boring, but I like it when they teach new material."

Sui Zi thought it was cute how Sung Tha Chin talked like a nine-year-old adult. When they came to the place in the camp where Sui Zi gave Burmese lessons, they sat down to talk. Sui Zi quizzed Sung Tha Chin on many subjects and found her to be far ahead of her fourth grade class. She was very bright, even with all of her little quirks. She bit her lips a lot and did not make any eye contact with Sui Zi even though she was completely engaged in the conversation. Sui Zi wondered if Sung Tha Chin had some form of autism. Soon it was time for Sui Zi to walk Sung Tha Chin back to her room at the camp. Sung Tha Chin told her she could find her way back, but Sui Zi told her she would enjoy accompanying her.

When they got back to the family, Sui Zi asked if she could talk with Sung Tha Chin's father in private. He went outside with Sui Zi, and they discussed Sung Tha Chin at length. The father said, "I am having difficulty with my new wife; she does not accept Sung Tha Chin. Her grandparents are all too old to care for her, or I would place her with them. We do not have funds to send Sung Tha Chin away to school. My wife is not cruel to Sung Tha Chin; she just doesn't want to care for her as her own child. She resents that it takes resources from our other children. It is a strain on our marriage and not good for Sung Tha Chin. She is unique and different from the other children. She obsesses and talks about things that interest her for hours, but if something does not interest her, it is difficult to get her to pay attention or do another activity."

Sui Zi told him about the children's home that she worked with in Mandalay. "It is a Christian home where the children are taught not only their studies but also about Jesus."

The father immediately expressed interest in sending Sung Tha Chin there.

Sui Zi said, "I will talk with Pastor Bawi, and we will work out a time for Sung Tha Chin to join the children's home."

"Thank you, thank you. Because I cannot afford to send Sung Tha Chin away to school, this will greatly please my wife."

Sui Zi and Pastor Bawi agreed that Sung Tha Chin could come the next month. Sui Zi continued to see her at the refugee camp and discuss English and Burmese with her. She told her all about the children's home. "You will have the opportunity to go to school and have tuition classes."

"Oh, but all I want to learn is how to speak English and Burmese. I get bored with the rest of school." Sung Tha Chin was quite emphatic.

Sui Zi explained, "You need the other classes and must do your best to pass so that one day you can go to the university." Sui Zi discovered that Sung Tha Chin was very interested in going to the university. "You could get any job you want if you go to the university."

Sung Tha Chin asked, "If that includes studying and becoming an English teacher, I will do it. I want to go to England or America and practice my English."

Sui Zi told her about the trip to the children's home and things they would do on the way. She said, "At the children's home you will have many friends, activities, and excellent food."

"Do the other girls know English?" Sung Tha Chin wanted to know.

"English is required at school, so yes, other children will be able to practice English with you."

The month went fast and soon Sui Zi was standing with Sung Tha Chin as she said goodbye to her father, grandparents, brother, and sister. Her stepmother stood back and did not engage in the farewells. Sung Tha Chin finally turned and took Sui Zi's hand, and they walked through the refugee camp one last time. They got into the taxi to go to Sui Zi's house where they would spend the night. Early in the morning they would catch the train to Mandalay.

At Sui Zi's house, Sung Tha Chin was interested in their two rooms and watched with great interest as Sui Zi prepared their evening meal. Sung Tha Chin ate a generous amount of food; having three good meals a day along with snacks at the children's home would be healthy for this girl. She ate three helpings for dinner. Then she said, "I have not had fried chicken in a long time; it is my favorite food. Will we have fried chicken at the children's home?"

"Absolutely. On occasion you will have fried chicken; the cook is very good at the home. I wish I had some chicken to fry for our trip to the home, but I do not." After Sung Tha Chin was asleep, Sui Zi called Pastor Bawi and requested fried chicken for their first dinner at the children's home.

"Should we wait a few days for Sung Tha Chin to have an appetite?" he asked.

Sui Zi laughed and said, "That will not be a problem. The child just had three helpings of rice, beef, vegetables, and dahl for dinner."

Morning came and Sung Tha Chin wanted to look her best, so she wore her best shirt that was her favorite color of blue, with pants and sandals for their trip. Sui Zi combed her short hair, and she looked very nice. They ate a quick breakfast, and once again Sung Tha Chin ate generously; then off to the train they went. Sui Zi's husband told them goodbye and wished Sung Tha Chin well. He told Sui Zi he would pray for her travel and be there to pick her up when she returned. They stood on the train platform and waited for their train. Sui Zi prayed that Sung Tha Chin would not have motion sickness as some children did on the long train ride.

Soon they were on their way to Mandalay. Thankfully, Sung Tha Chin did not have motion sickness. She had the opposite problem – she wanted to eat constantly. Sui Zi bought her popcorn, and they ate out of their lunch tins at the first stop. At the second stop, she bought Sung Tha Chin her first ice cream.

Sung Tha Chin declared, "I love this ice cream! Will we have it at the children's home?"

At the third stop, they ate another full meal. Sui Zi thought

Sung Tha Chin was making up for years of not eating well. She wondered if the stepmother had denied her food in order to have enough for her own two children.

After the third stop, Sung Tha Chin laid her head on Sui Zi and fell sound asleep for the rest of the train ride. When they arrived, Sui Zi greeted her old friend Pastor Bawi and introduced him to Sung Tha Chin. Since he knew she loved English, he greeted her by saying, "Hello, how are you?" in English.

She quickly answered, "Fine, thank you, and how are you?"

"You speak English very well," he told her. This earned another smile. They walked to the cab that was waiting for them, and Pastor Bawi was well on his way to building a relationship with Sung Tha Chin.

When they reached the children's home, all the children ran out to meet Sung Tha Chin. One of the girls, Nila, who was also nine years old, came over and introduced herself to Sung Tha Chin. She asked if she could show her their room. Then she said, "I would like to be your friend and show you around the home."

Sung Tha Chin surprised Sui Zi by letting go of her hand and walking off with Nila while asking if she spoke English. Sui Zi followed as Nila showed her their room, Sung Tha Chin's bed, and a place to store her things. Nila explained what Sung Tha Chin needed to do to be registered. "You will go and have your picture taken and then see the doctor."

"Why do I have to have my picture taken?"

Nila explained, "All the children who live here have their pictures taken by the army, so they know who lives here."

"I've never seen a doctor," Sung Tha Chin told Nila. They discussed the doctor at great length, and Sung Tha Chin found a new topic of interest.

She asked Sui Zi when she would get to see the doctor.

"Within the week, Pastor Bawi and the house mother will take you to see the doctor."

Sung Tha Chin had lots of questions about doctors and how they made sickness go away. "Could a doctor make my *a phua*'s sickness go away?"

"That depends on what sickness your *a phua* has. I will see if a doctor can see her when I get back to the refugee camp."

By dinnertime, Sung Tha Chin had worked up quite an appetite. Nila had taught her how to make a jump rope out of rubber bands, and the two girls spent over an hour jumping rope and playing before dinner. Sung Tha Chin was excited to see her first meal was fried chicken with vegetables and rice. She again ate very well. Pastor Bawi joked with Sui Zi that Sung Tha Chin might increase their food budget if she kept eating as much as she was. He agreed that she must have been underfed, but he didn't want her to make herself sick by eating so much.

When it was time for Sui Zi to head over to Pastor Bawi's house with him, she made sure Sung Tha Chin knew she was leaving. It surprised her at how well Sung Tha Chin was acclimating to the home. That made her glad, because she was eager to go and see Seng Nu. Pastor Bawi told her to be prepared to meet a totally different child.

As they arrived at Pastor Bawi's house, she was greeted first by his wife and then his mother-in-law. Then in came Seng Nu carrying Siang Za Nawl with a huge smile on her face. She greeted Sui Zi and said, "I am very grateful to be living here in this family."

Sui Zi could not believe the radiant young girl in front of her was the same girl she had brought there three months ago. She was engaged like a member of the family, helping, talking, and smiling. She told Sui Zi, "I am enjoying school and have several friends. I also have fun playing badminton with my friends."

They discussed school and many topics for an hour as Seng

Nu sat on the floor and played with Siang Za Nawl. Sui Zi noticed the pallor was gone from her face, and her cheeks were fuller. She had gained a little weight and looked rested and at peace. They discussed church, and Seng Nu told her she loved to sing worship songs in church. Soon they said good-night, and Sui Zi went to sleep, praising God for rescuing these precious girls. The transformation of Seng Nu was truly a miracle.

In the morning, Sui Zi smiled as Seng Nu helped prepare the family's breakfast. Pastor Bawi and Sui Zi discussed politics and news from Chin State and Mandalay. Sui Zi wanted to get back to the children's home to see how Sung Tha Chin was getting along. Pastor Bawi told her not to be concerned; he was sure Sung Tha Chin was in good hands. When they headed over to the home, they found Sung Tha Chin in tuition class, looking bored. Sui Zi went in and asked her to come out and talk. Sung Tha Chin told her, "Tuition class is boring. I do not see any reason to memorize subjects."

Pastor Bawi smiled as he listened to Sung Tha Chin talk. He calmly interrupted and said, "Some subjects must be memorized in order to pass the end-of-year exams. It is important to do your best so you can move to the next grade and learn more subjects and new things. These are the government's rules for going to school, and you must do your very best."

Sung Tha Chin seemed to look right through Pastor Bawi and Sui Zi as they talked, but they knew she heard every word. They told her they were going to take her to the doctor after lunch and that she should eat quickly to be ready to go.

When lunchtime came, Sung Tha Chin ate very fast because she was interested in going to the doctor. At the clinic, the doctor examined her and confirmed what they suspected. Sung Tha Chin was about fifteen pounds underweight but was otherwise healthy.

He said, "From her reactions and speech, I think she has

autism. She was interested in everything I did and asked many questions, like, 'What did the eye chart tell you?' and 'Can I listen to my heart? What do you look for in my ears and mouth?'" She spoke like a nine-year-old adult, and the doctor was very patient with her. She asked him what she could do to become a doctor.

He told her, "You must do very well in your studies and go to the university for many years to learn to be a doctor."

Sui Zi could tell that Sung Tha Chin was taking all of this in. Maybe English would soon be replaced with an obsession for learning medicine.

Next, they took Sung Tha Chin to the authorities; this made her very nervous. The only authority she knew was the military from the war in Chin State, so she was very stoic and wouldn't smile for her picture. It was done quickly and with ease, for Pastor Bawi made sure to have friends among the local officials to help it go well for the children and the home.

As they traveled back to the home, Sung Tha Chin talked nonstop about becoming a doctor and what she would have to learn. Pastor Bawi told her, "You will have to do very well in all your school subjects and work hard to pass your exams to get done with school and go to the university."

The weekend went fast and soon Sui Zi was saying goodbye to Pastor Bawi's family and all of the precious children she had brought to them. As they drove to the railroad station, Sui Zi and Pastor Bawi continued to share stories about the children.

Sui Zi said, "I am thankful for this mission and to be involved in it with you. I'm thankful for all the children we've rescued too."

Pastor Bawi added, "One of the boys will be leaving for the university, so there is room for another boy. If you know of one, please let me know."

Soon Sui Zi was on the train heading back home. She spent

most of the trip resting or praying for the children and thanking God that they were doing so well, especially Seng Nu. She fell asleep wondering if Sung Tha Chin would become an English teacher or a doctor, and thankful that she now had the opportunity to become either one; she could have hope and a future through Jesus Christ.

Thang Duh Lian

A ten-year-old boy named Thang Duh Lian, somewhat reserved but doting over his baby brother, lived in a village with his mother, stepfather, and little brother. They fled out of the mountains from the government and rebel fighting and relocated to a village a few hours from the main fighting area. They attended a Christian Church there and enjoyed listening to the pastor who was one of the pastors Sui Zi knew and worked with to help relocate at-risk or orphaned children.

Thang Duh Lian's mother spoke to the pastor. "I am concerned for my son and do not want him taken away and forced to fight as a child soldier. He is young and quiet and not a fighter. We relocated to get away from the fighting and to protect him. We had been rice farmers in the mountains but had to move frequently. Thang Duh Lian has a third grade education; we have tried to keep him in school."

The pastor responded, "I know of a Christian children's home that takes orphaned children and provides an education for them. They would protect him and not allow him to be forced into military service as a child soldier"

Thang Duh Lian's mother said, "My son is somewhat outcast by my husband. He has not accepted him because he is his stepfather. The two of them have a difficult time together. I will pray and think about possibly moving the boy to the children's home. I am only concerned that I may not see him again since my husband likes to move and keep busy farming."

The pastor called Sui Zi to tell her they might have a new boy to rescue out of the fighting and to ask her to join them in praying for the direction God wanted for this young boy. He told her about Thang Duh Lian. "He is a pleasant boy who loves church. He is attentive during worship services and has never missed a Sunday since moving into the village with his family. He loves talking with me and he loves Jesus. The mother says the stepfather ignores the child. He would need tutoring since he is a couple years behind in school."

"I will notify Pastor Bawi that there is a potential new child and will be in prayer for the family's decision," she told him.

Within a day the stepfather came to the pastor and said they would like to send Thang Duh Lian to the children's home. The mother did not look up at the pastor as this was announced, so he asked her if she was sure. She softly replied, "It will be safer for the boy; I do not want him pressed into military service. He is a gentle boy who loves the Lord. This way he will have a chance for an education."

The pastor felt for Thang Duh Lian's mother and reassured her. "I will stay in touch with the team that rescues the Christian children. As long as you stay near my village, I will be able to give you updates on how he is doing. Sui Zi, a co-worker with the children's home, keeps track of the children they have rescued and always gives me updates on them."

Two weeks later the pastor and Thang Duh Lian were on their way to Sui Zi's town. Sui Zi was glad when they arrived. She and her husband had been praying for Thang Duh Lian and that he would make it safely out of the war zone. He was a precious boy with a beautiful light in his brown eyes. Sui Zi was glad they were rescuing him. They planned to spend the night at her apartment and then start their train ride the next day.

The group piled in Ja San's taxi and headed to the apartment. Sui Zi had prepared a simple dinner of chicken, vegetables, rice, and dahl. Thang Duh Lian was obviously very hungry from the trip, for he ate several servings. After dinner he looked tired, so Sui Zi set him up with a mat and got him ready for bed. He was sound asleep in a few minutes.

Thang Duh Lian slept soundly through the night, and Sui Zi hated to wake him in the morning. She gently wiggled his shoulder until he woke up and waited as he adjusted to where he was. Then she asked if he would like some food before they started their trip. He got up and quickly got ready for the day. He ate a good breakfast but then asked Sui Zi if they could pray for his mother and little brother – and his step-father too – before they left. She loved this boy's heart and that he had asked to pray. She obliged him and prayed for their travel and his family.

Soon they were back in Ja San's cab and headed to the train station for the fourteen-hour trip. At the train station, they sat on a bench and waited for the train. Ja San wished them safe travels and told Thang Duh Lian that he enjoyed meeting him and would be praying for him. Fortunately, the train was on time, and Sui Zi found a seat for them by a window. Thang Duh Lian asked if he could sit closest to the window. As they traveled, he was interested in seeing the different villages and changing land. He took in all the sights of the city also, and Sui Zi pointed out different sights to him. He had spent his whole life in the mountain villages, and the city had much to hold his attention.

Sui Zi made sure the trip was fun for Thang Duh Lian and was glad that he did not seem to miss his family. Instead, he seemed excited to be going. He had his first popcorn and ice cream as they traveled through the train stations and managed to empty the lunch buckets that Sui Zi had packed for them with the leftover chicken, vegetables, rice, and dahl. In the afternoon Sui Zi asked him about his life in the mountain villages.

"We moved a lot to different areas to plant rice. I carried things on my back when we moved. My job at home was to chop down small pine trees and cut the trunks into many pieces to burn in our hut for light in the evenings. I like the smell of the pine, but it is so sticky. I would also gather firewood for my mother's cooking fire."

"When I was a girl, growing up in the village," Sui Zi told him, "I can remember waking up with soot all over my face from our cooking fires."

Thang Duh Lian laughed and said he had it up his nose too, and they both shared a good laugh. After a long day of travel, they arrived at the Mandalay train station. Pastor Bawi waved as the train pulled in and came to a stop. Sui Zi loved this young pastor and his heart to save children. She always smiled and waved back as they came into the station.

Pastor Bawi got down to eye level and greeted Thang Duh Lian. "I am so glad to meet you; I have been praying for you. How was your trip? Do you need anything?"

Thang Duh Lian responded with a handshake and a soft, "No, thank you."

Then they climbed into a taxi and rode to the children's home. Pastor Bawi pointed out various sights and showed Thang Duh Lian where he and his family lived. Then he explained that the children's home used to be in the apartments, but he was a lucky boy because now they had a brand-new home for the children. When they arrived at Hope Christian Children's Home, Seng Awn Lungjung and all the children ran out to greet Thang Duh Lian.

This was the first time Sui Zi saw Thang Duh Lian hesitate. All the children and the large new children's home might have been a bit overwhelming for him. Pastor Bawi quickly put his arm around Thang Duh Lian and escorted him past the children, making introductions as they went. Pastor Bawi called for Mang Lian Hup to come and greet Thang Duh Lian. Mang Lian Hup came up and started talking away to Thang Duh Lian in their native language. This was a great surprise, but Sui Zi knew that Thang Duh Lian would have to learn Burmese quickly now that he lived in the city.

Pastor Bawi had tea and dinner waiting for them. Sui Zi enjoyed having dinner at the new children's home and seeing how beautiful and fully operational it was now. During the meal she glanced over at Thang Duh Lian. He was smiling and talking with a few boys who also came from his area.

Pastor Bawi was glad to show Sui Zi all the children and tell her how they were doing. She was especially glad to hear that Seng Nu continued to do well. Soon they took Thang Duh Lian to his bed, which was in the same room as Mang Lian Hup. Thang Duh Lian settled in, and Sui Zi and Pastor Bawi wished him a good night's sleep.

Sui Zi would spend the night at Pastor Bawi's house. They had much to discuss regarding the move of Pastor Bawi's nephew

Khuang Ja and niece Numri Pan to the home next month. Even though it had been a long day of travel, Pastor Bawi and his family kept Sui Zi up for three more hours, sharing news and planning the big surprise that would happen when school ended. Pastor Bawi, Sui Zi, and Mang Lian Hup's village pastor had all saved up funds to bring Mang Lian Hup's *a phua* to Mandalay to visit for six weeks. The *a phua* had been in contact with Sui Zi and Pastor Bawi several times over the past school year, inquiring about Mang Lian Hup and wanting to see him. Three churches all worked together to gather the funds to bring her for a visit. It would be a big surprise for Mang Lian Hup and a blessing for his *a phua*.

In the morning, Sui Zi went with Pastor Bawi to talk with Thang Duh Lian and discuss some of the things he would have to do in the next couple of days – the visit with the doctor and government officials. He still had a month before school started, but tuition classes could begin to prepare him for next year. He would start in fourth grade, even though his age placed him in sixth grade. Sui Zi favored the fourth grade start, but they would assess that further in his tuition classes.

As Pastor Bawi talked with Thang Duh Lian, he got a huge compliment from him when Thang Duh Lian said he would like to grow up and be a pastor like him. When Pastor Bawi asked him why he wanted to be a pastor, Thang Duh Lian answered, "To share the love of Jesus with other people and help explain to them what Jesus did for us on the cross, how Jesus saved us."

The day and night passed quickly, and Sui Zi had one last breakfast at the children's home before heading to the train station. During breakfast Pastor Bawi said to Thang Duh Lian, "Could you please share your favorite Bible verse with us?"

Thang Duh Lian without hesitation recited Psalm 23:

"The Lord is my shepherd; I lack nothing.

He makes me lie down in green pastures, he leads me beside quiet waters,

he refreshes my soul. He guides me along the right paths for his name's sake.

Even though I walk through the darkest valley, I will fear no evil, for you are with me; your rod and your staff, they comfort me.

You prepare a table before me in the presence of my enemies. You anoint my head with oil; my cup overflows.

Surely your goodness and love will follow me all the days of my life, and I will dwell in the house of the Lord forever."

Mang Lian Hup's A Phua

School ended and Sui Zi prepared for the big trip to get Mang Lian Hup's *a phua*. The plan was for Sui Zi to go to the strawberry farms and bring her to her home for two days. Then she would take Mang Lian Hup's *a phua*, Khuang Ja, and his sister Numri Pan to Mandalay. As Sui Zi prepared for this trip, it had seemed so far in the future, but suddenly the time had come. She told her husband that morning that it felt like time went faster and faster the older she got. She planned to spend two weeks at the children's home and assist in some of the Burmese tuition classes. Her husband would miss her during this time, but he knew she loved her mission work with the children of Myanmar, and he knew how precious the children were to her.

The trip to the strawberry farms was peaceful, and unlike the last time when Sui Zi arrived, Mang Lian Hup's *a phua* was all smiles and excited to see her grandson. She was packed and ready to go when Sui Zi arrived. While they had tea at the village pastor's hut, Mang Lian Hup's *a phua* expressed that she was overwhelmed by the outpouring of the three churches that had taken special offerings to send her to see Mang Lian Hup. Sui Zi told her it was her insistence on seeing her grandson and God's blessing that was enabling this trip. The *a phua* would stay at Hope Christian Children's Home for six weeks and travel back from Mandalay by herself since Sui Zi could not stay that long. Then Sui Zi and her husband would take her back to the strawberry farms.

During the trip to Sui Zi's home, the *a phua* talked constantly about Mang Lian Hup and barely gave Sui Zi time to answer a question before she asked the next question. She was pleased to hear that he was helping other children adjust to living at the home when they arrived and that he still wore the necklace she had given him when he left.

Sui Zi told her how much Mang Lian Hup had grown and that he was doing well in his studies. The *a phua* had not traveled outside the surrounding areas of her village for many years, so the many buildings, cars, trucks, and busy people struck her with awe. At Sui Zi's apartment, she was interested in the layout and especially the kitchen. She asked many questions as Sui Zi prepared their evening meal without using a fire.

"Tomorrow," Sui Zi explained, "I will be working with the two children who are moving to the children's home. They will travel with us. Khuang Ja and his sister Numri Pan are moving there to attend secondary school."

The *a phua* said, "No one in my family has gone to secondary school; I am pleased that Mang Lian Hup will be able to do so."

The next day Sui Zi helped Khuang Ja and his sister pack; then she gathered supplies that Pastor Bawi had requested, hoping she could get them cheaper in her area of Myanmar.

Khuang Ja and Numri Pan found it hard to say goodbye to their sister, mother, and father that evening. Due to the early start the next day, Sui Zi took them to her apartment for the night. Khuang Ja hugged his dad and promised he would get his education and then come back and help care for them. Numri Pan was very quiet and asked her mother if she was sure she should go. Her mother told her yes, she needed to get her education finished so she could have a good job. After many hugs and tears, the children left with Sui Zi.

At Sui Zi's apartment, everyone helped her pack the supplies they were taking to the school and then turned in for a good night's sleep. Khuang Ja and Numri Pan were the first to fall asleep. Sui Zi was not sure, but she thought she heard Numri Pan crying. She left her alone. It was hard to leave your home for the unknown, even if she would be staying with a relative; it was still not home with her parents. Mang Lian Hup's *a phua* was so excited Sui Zi feared she would not sleep. She told her, "Please sleep. Tomorrow we have a long journey to Mandalay."

Sui Zi packed four lunch pails for the long trip and made sure she had plenty of funds for the train tickets, drinks, and snacks along the route. She then double-checked her bag to make sure she had all she needed for two weeks away from home. Then finally, she went to sleep herself.

The morning was busy with cooking a nice breakfast and getting the children ready for the long trip ahead. Mang Lian Hup's *a phua* was excited and the first one ready to get going. She told the children, "Many years ago I took a long train ride to visit my aunt and uncle. Now I am excited to travel again to see my grandson."

Ja San loaded his taxi and took all of them to the train station. This time they were not lucky; they had a two-hour wait for the train to arrive. Sui Zi called Pastor Bawi to let him know they would be running late. Finally, when everyone was settled on the train, they were off for the long ride to Mandalay.

The ride started out quietly, but soon the children and *A Phua* were thrilled at what they saw out the window and exclaimed at the sights. They all enjoyed snacks sold by vendors who came through the train cars. At their lunch stop, they finished the food in their lunch pails that Sui Zi had packed for them. Khuang Ja was pleased that Sui Zi had remembered his favorite food was eggs and that she had packed a couple hard-boiled eggs in his lunch pail.

During the afternoon both children fell asleep, and Sui Zi talked with the *a phua*. She was eager for information about their country and the children's home. At the next train stop, Sui Zi bought everyone ice cream. Mang Lian Hup's *a phua* had never had ice cream and was delighted with the cold treat. After a long day of travel, they finally pulled into the Mandalay train station at dusk. Pastor Bawi was there to greet them – along with Mang Lian Hup.

Khuang Ja and Numri Pan were pleased to see their uncle when they arrived. Mang Lian Hup's *a phua* cried tears of joy when she saw her precious grandson waving and standing tall by Pastor Bawi's side. Eventually they emerged from the train, and Mang Lian Hup ran into his *a phua*'s arms for a long embrace. They spoke in their native language while Pastor Bawi greeted his niece and nephew. "We must hurry along; it is getting very late. I have some food for you for your dinner."

They all climbed into two cabs for the trip to Hope Christian Children's Home. Sui Zi, Mang Lian Hup, and his *a phua* rode

MANG LIAN HUP'S A PHUA

in one cab while Pastor Bawi, Khuang Ja, and Numri Pan were in the other. When they reached the children's home, Pastor Bawi moved them along to the dining area. Mang Lian Hup was excited and wanted to show everything to his *a phua*, and the children had all gathered to meet the new arrivals. It was quite a busy moment. Sui Zi was pleased to see Seng Nu with Pastor Bawi's wife, ready to serve their meal and happy to see them. The change in the girl that Sui Zi had first brought to the home continued to amaze her.

Pastor Bawi gave thanks before they ate. He praised God for their safe travel and thanked Him for providing the funds for Mang Lian Hup's *a phua* to come and be with them. When everyone finished dinner, it was very late. Pastor Bawi gave Mang Lian Hup instructions. "There will be plenty of time to show your *a phua* around the home; I'd like you to go and help her get settled in her room at the home. She will share a room with the school cook."

Once the *a phua* was settled, she went up to see where Mang Lian Hup slept and told him good-night. When both of them were settled, Sui Zi and Pastor Bawi went to check on Khuang Ja and Numri Pan. His wife had helped set them up in their rooms with their new friends. Khuang Ja had chosen an empty top bunk bed for his bed and had already unpacked his things into his locker. They found Numri Pan sitting on a lower bunk that she had chosen as she talked with two other girls. She still needed to unpack, and Pastor Bawi told the girls that it was late, and they should get ready for sleep. He reminded them that they had early-morning tuition classes the next day.

Soon Sui Zi, Seng Nu, Pastor Bawi, and his wife were headed for their apartment. Everyone was tired, and it was not long before they were all lying on their mats asleep.

The next day was very busy. When they arrived at the children's home, they found Mang Lian Hup's *a phua* helping in the kitchen while Mang Lian Hup was in his tuition classes. Pastor Bawi told her to please rest, but she insisted on helping. "I am so very grateful for how healthy and happy Mang Lian Hup is to be living in the children's home that the least I can do is help out while he is busy in classes."

Sui Zi wandered around the home while Pastor Bawi attended to the home's business work. She found all the children that she had brought to Hope Christian Children's Home during the last couple of years – Mang Lian Hup, Mai Jar, Mala, Khuang Ja, Numri Pan, Lang Meng, Cin Vang, Seng Nu, Sung Tha Chin, and Thang Duh Lian – in their respective tuition classes.

Sui Zi sat for a while in each class and listened to the children recite their lessons. She was pleased to see all of the precious children she had brought there doing well. She spent time going over their grades and files with Seng Awn Lungjung, the home's director, before she headed home. Knowing how they were doing helped her when anyone asked about them. Ja San also liked to hear about the children because he cared about the mission work of rescuing the children in Chin and Kachin States.

After Sui Zi listened to the children's various tuition classes, she headed to Pastor Bawi's office to meet with him and have tea. They discussed the children, the needs of the home, and politics. Pastor Bawi took Sui Zi for a walk to an area next to the children's home. "I am praying for God's direction about buying this piece of land. I think it could be used to expand an area for the children to play in and to build a home for my family close to the children's home. We are getting a bit full in our apartment with my wife, children, the three girls, and mother-in-law all living in that one apartment. Three girls, including Seng Nu, do not want to live in the children's home and prefer to be with us. I don't want to force them to live in the home. If they need to be close to my family, that is fine with me and my wife, but it makes for tight living arrangements."

"I will pray for God's will about the purchase of the land and the building of a home," Sui Zi told Pastor Bawi. "It would be nice to have some room for the children to play too. If they want to play futball or volleyball now, they have to play in the street. It would be safer to be in a designated area for play."

Sui Zi left Hope Christian Children's Home for a couple days in the middle of her stay in order to travel and check on the children at Grace Christian Children's Home. She enjoyed leaving the business of the slum area where Hope Christian Children's Home was located for the peace and quiet of the more rural Grace Christian Children's Home. On the way to the home, she passed beautiful golden pagodas, and she thought about how many people called Myanmar the Golden Land because of all the golden pagodas. As they drove along the rivers, she saw huts on stilts and long tail boats.

They came to the road that led to Grace Christian Children's Home. The driver did not think his car could safely go up the dirt road, so he dropped Sui Zi off at the end of the road and promised to be back in two days at midday to return her to Hope Christian Children's Home. A homeowner happened by with a cart and offered to load her belongings and supplies and pull it to the children's home. As they walked up the road, Sui Zi thought the car driver over-reacted. It was dry and not muddy with very few ruts. She believed the car could have made it with only getting a little extra dust on it. She enjoyed the walk outside nevertheless.

At Grace, her friends who ran the home greeted her with tea. Dua Lian Hmung came for tea with the other children. He brought his guitar because he was eager to play some new songs he had learned for Sui Zi. All the children waited patiently, even though they expected Sui Zi to open her bag and pass out gifts to them. She had brought rubber bands, marbles, barrettes, a futball, and a new volleyball/badminton set for the children. Then Sui Zi watched the children break into groups to play. Some boys played with rubber bands, and others played with marbles or the futball. Some of the girls fixed their hair with barrettes while others played volleyball; by the side of the net, other girls played badminton. Sui Zi complimented everyone on the thriving garden. They all agreed this was a good way for the home to grow vegetables for the children.

However, Sui Zi was upset when she heard that the home had had a series of break-ins by migrant workers from the neighboring farms. Most had been crimes of opportunity – stealing tools or toys that they had left outside unattended. The biggest loss was two of their bikes that the staff used to get to market. They were working with the Myanmar sponsor and the new U.S. sponsor, Child Help International, to get the funds to build a wall around the property.

Sui Zi could not imagine who would steal from widows and orphans, and she promised to pray for the funds needed to build the wall and continue to pray for the funds to repair the children's buildings. She had brought extra money to assist with any needs that the homes had, and she decided that getting two bikes for the home would assist the widows who ran the home to get their errands done. She gave them the money, and they promised they would buy the bikes and keep them in the main building to discourage another theft.

Running a children's home was an expensive undertaking, and this home relied heavily on the Myanmar and U.S. sponsors for support. Sui Zi was thankful that a U.S. nonprofit, Child Help International, had recently become involved with both Hope and Grace Christian Children's Homes. Child Help International could find sponsors for the children and run building/repair campaigns. Sui Zi knew these funds would be put to good use in support of the children and the homes. She was also thankful that the churches of the world worked to help the widows and children.

Sui Zi went back to Hope Christian Children's Home and spent the rest of her time helping in tuition classes and visiting with her good friends at the home. On her last day before traveling home, Mang Lian Hup's *a phua* asked if they could speak. "Would you speak to Pastor Bawi to see if I could stay at the children's home? I would be pleased to be a cleaning lady and help take care of all the children."

Sui Zi approached Pastor Bawi with this idea. He said, "Unfortunately, the home staff positions are all full, but it is a good idea. Let's meet with the *a phua*, and if a position at the home should open up, I will consider bringing her back to work at the home, but at this time the home staff positions are all full."

The *a phua* was disappointed but she understood. The possibility of a position opening up gave her hope of coming back in the future. They agreed to pray for God's will concerning her move when a position came available.

Sui Zi woke early and was all packed for her return trip home. She and Pastor Bawi began the taxi ride to the train station. As always, Pastor Bawi stayed with Sui Zi until the train arrived. This time the train was only ten minutes late. Before Sui Zi boarded, Pastor Bawi prayed for her travel, work, and husband. Sui Zi settled onto the train and waved goodbye to her good friend as the train pulled away from Mandalay. Sui Zi smiled at the memories of this trip. It was good to see the children thriving at both of the children's homes. She would be glad to share the updates with her husband and the Myanmar Christian churches that helped support these homes. She prayed a prayer of thanksgiving for all the blessings God had bestowed on these children and thanked Him for calling her to work with His Precious Children of Myanmar.

Child Help International

My husband, Bruce, and I have been blessed to be partners with Child Help International since our first storytelling mission trip to Kenya. When we got the opportunity to go with Child Help International as they began their work in Myanmar with these two children's homes, we were excited to once again partner with our brother in Christ, Nate Banta. Child Help International helps support both the Grace and Hope Christian Children's Homes. Our sponsors were able to send enough support with us that we could provide more sports equipment for each children's home, build a well for clean water for the slum and Hope Christian Children's Home, and repair all the floorboards and the porch at Grace Christian Children's Home.

Currently Child Help International assists national churches in Kenya, Myanmar, and India to run Christian children's homes and rescue centers. These homes employ widows as caregivers for the children, house mothers, and cooks. Each home has a local church to support the home, a pastor who runs the home, and a director to help with the day-to-day operations. You can support Child Help International through prayer, donations, child sponsorship, or mission trips to visit with the children. They also run CHI Coffee near Boise, Idaho, to help support the projects.

Nate and Stacy (our US representatives) and their children,

Daniel, Miriam, and Micah, are extended family to us, and we are always with them in prayer as they work around the world to rescue orphans and street children in the name of Jesus Christ.

Support for the Mission Featured in
Precious Children of Myanmar

To contact or support Child Help International:

Website: www.childhelpinternational.com

Email: nate@childhelpinternational.com

Mail: Child Help International
1803 S. 10th Ave.
Caldwell, ID 83605

All names of Child Help International personnel in Myanmar and the children have been changed to protect their identities.

About the Author

Elizabeth Carpenter and her husband, Bruce, have been deeply touched by the desperate needs of children around the world. They answered God's call to give these children a voice by gathering and sharing their stories. From this calling, His Precious Children: A Story-Sharing Ministry was formed. Their ongoing passion is to work with needy children around the world and empower them by telling their stories. Their most recent trip was to Myanmar.

Elizabeth and Bruce live in Ohio with their dogs, Zoey and Lexi. They have two grown children – a daughter, Christina (husband Brian), and a son, Zachary (wife Jessica), and Elizabeth's youngest brother, Kevin (wife Jessie), who is like a son. They love being grandparents to Ethan, Oliver, Piper, and Tucker. They are part of the church family at Discover Christian Church in Dublin, Ohio.

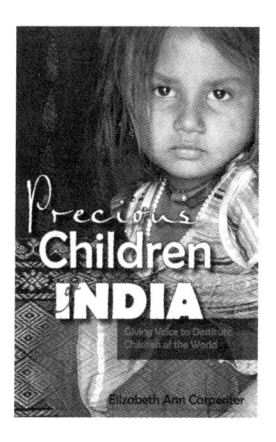

Precious Children of India

Children around the world live in dire conditions without even the basic necessities of water, food, shelter, and love. They often suffer in silence, struggling just to exist among the unexplainable and irreversible conditions in which they find themselves. Many are so young they do not know what they lack – the love of a family and the comfort of a home. Survival is their only concern as they grow up in a world of adults who seem to have forgotten them or are so busy with their own survival that they really do not have time to care.

These first person narratives are compiled from conversations with dozens of boys and girls in India. They put a voice to the suffering that they and thousands more like them endure every day. Children bravely share their stories of being caste bound, trafficked, beggars, witnesses to murder, unwanted, and of suffering great loss. Each child is a witness to his or her own story of survival. From their voices can be heard the desperate plea for someone to care, and if not for themselves, then for those even less fortunate whose voices have not been heard.

Available where books are sold.

Precious Children of Kenya

Children around the world live in dire conditions without even the basic necessities of water, food, shelter, and love. They often suffer in silence, struggling just to exist among the unexplainable and irreversible conditions in which they find themselves. Many are so young that they do not know what they lack - the love of a family and the comfort of a home. Survival is their only concern. They grow up in a world of adults who seem to have forgotten them, or are so busy with their own survival that they really do not have time to care. These first-person narratives are compiled from conversations with dozens of boys and girls in Kenya, Africa. They put a voice to the suffering that they and thousands more like them endure every day. In towns, villages and desert huts, children tell about living through abandonment, abuse, slavery, and loss of parents and family members due to AIDS, ethnic clashes, and illness caused by starvation or malaria. Each child is a witness to his or her own story of survival. Through their voices can be heard the desperate plea for someone to possibly care, if not for themselves, then for those even less fortunate whose voices have not been heard.

Available where books are sold.